MYSTERIOUS PLACES
THE MAGICAL EAST

MYSTERIOUS PLACES
THE MAGICAL EAST

Philip Wilkinson & Michael Pollard

Illustrations by Robert Ingpen

DRAGON'S
WORLD

Dragon's World Ltd
Limpsfield
Surrey RH8 0DY
Great Britain

First published by Dragon's World 1992

© Text by Dragon's World 1992
© Illustrations by Robert Ingpen 1990 & 1992

Simplified text and captions by **Michael Pollard**
based on the *Encyclopedia of Mysterious Places*
by Robert Ingpen and Philip Wilkinson.

Editor	Diana Briscoe
Designer	Design 23
Art Director	Dave Allen
Editorial Director	Pippa Rubinstein

**British Library Cataloguing
in Publication Data**
The catalogue record for this book is
available from the British Library.

ISBN 1 80528 178 5

Printed in Italy.

CONTENTS

Introduction

Nowadays we are very used to hearing about the Far East. Many of the things we use, from Japanese hi-fi to Chinese toys, come from there. We can hear about events in India and Japan on the news almost every day of the week, and jet airliners make it quick and easy to travel there too.

But before this century the East was much more mysterious to the people of Europe and America. Travel to the East involved lengthy journeys by land or sea, with the risks of shipwreck or disease, pirates or bandits. The stories that the few travellers to China or India brought back described a life completely different from that in the West. The people wore strange costumes and worshipped unfamiliar gods; they were ruled by kings whose wealth seemed unparalleled.

The splendours of the East
In many ways the people of India and China, Japan and South-East Asia, seemed more advanced than those in the West. Travellers came back with stories of apparently magical devices like water clocks and compasses. They also told of great building feats, like the Great Wall that stretched all the way around the vast Chinese empire, and the enormous palace of the Chinese emperors – so vast that it was a city in its own right.

It was not just the great and powerful empire of China that contained such amazing buildings. Rumours came back of temples hewn out of the bare rock in India, great cities among the forests of Khampuchea, and a unique, closed civilisation in Japan. Further afield, cities like Great Zimbabwe in Africa surprised the people of Europe with their sophistication.

The time line to the right makes it easy for you to see at a glance which civilisations in this book came first and which came later. Along the top of the line are dates; you can tell from the length of the bars below how long or short a time the site was important. Look at the map to see where the sites are in relation to each other.

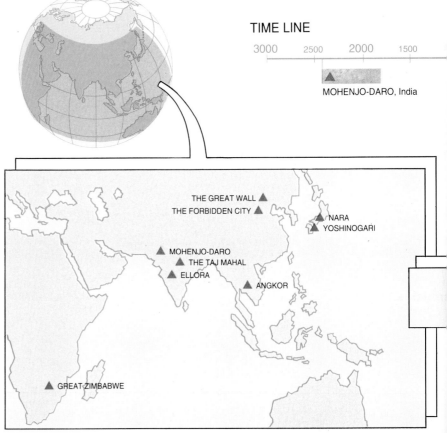

TIME LINE

3000	2500	2000	1500

MOHENJO-DARO, India

THE GREAT WALL ▲
THE FORBIDDEN CITY ▲

▲ NARA
▲ YOSHINOGARI

▲ MOHENJO-DARO
▲ THE TAJ MAHAL
▲ ELLORA

▲ ANGKOR

▲ GREAT ZIMBABWE

This book brings together some of the most interesting places of the Far East and beyond. It begins with some of the most ancient places of the East: the city of Mohenjo-Daro in India, the Great Wall of China and the mysterious site of Yoshinogari in Japan.

All these places are great beginnings. Mohenjo-Daro was the centre of what was probably the first Indian civilisation. Some archaeologists think that its people practised a primitive version of the Hindu religion. The Great Wall was the lasting achievement of the first emperor of China, the man who first united the country. The city of Yoshinogari may have been the headquarters of the ancestors of the later emperors of Japan.

Some of the other places in this book show civilisations at later stages in their story. The Buddhist temples of Nara bear witness to the refinement of civilisation in Japan. The superb craftsmanship of Ellora and the Taj Mahal show the variety of cultures that developed in India – Hindu, Buddhist, and Islamic, while the Forbidden City in Beijing was the headquarters of the later Chinese emperors.

The life of the places
Considering their great age, many of these buildings are still in surprisingly good condition. But they still keep their mystery, belonging for the most part to civilisations that have perished or changed beyond recognition. In this book we look at the peoples who lived in these places as well as the places themselves. The pictures in this book will show you their costumes and possessions; the text describes their beliefs and their legends.

We see the traders of Great Zimbabwe exchanging goods with merchants from Asia, the monks of Ellora meditating, the soldiers of Imperial China defending the wall against a barbarian invasion. We find out about the single-minded individuals who built the great palaces of Beijing or the Taj Mahal, and about the societies that created the temples of Angkor and the statues of Easter Island.

These places demonstrate the incredible diversity of life in the Far East. They show how the 'magic' of the East is still something we can marvel at, and help us to understand the character of the East we know today.

Philip Wilkinson

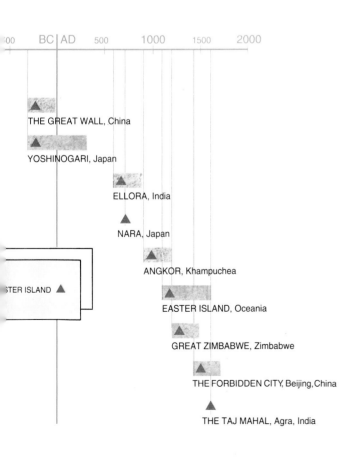

00   BC AD   500   1000   1500   2000

THE GREAT WALL, China

YOSHINOGARI, Japan

ELLORA, India

NARA, Japan

ANGKOR, Khampuchea

TER ISLAND

EASTER ISLAND, Oceania

GREAT ZIMBABWE, Zimbabwe

THE FORBIDDEN CITY, Beijing, China

THE TAJ MAHAL, Agra, India

Mohenjo-Daro

India, c. 2400–1800 BC

The people of Mohenjo-Daro depended on the river Indus for their prosperity. But in the end the river overwhelmed them, and in its last days their once magnificent city became a slum.

The Indus is one of the world's longest rivers. Rising in the mountains of Tibet, it flows for 3000 kilometres (1900 miles) south-westwards across a wide plain of fertile land (in what is now Pakistan) until it reaches the Arabian Sea.

Vanishing cities

Like the deltas of the Nile, the Tigris and the Euphrates, the lower valley of the Indus attracted settlers because of the richness of the soil. Farming prospered so well that by about 2400 BC the Indus Valley people had created the first great civilisation in the Indian sub-continent. It included a number of wealthy cities trading across the Arabian Sea.

Mohenjo-Daro, which at its peak was home for up to 40,000 people, was one of them. Yet Mohenjo-Daro, and at least seventy other sites of the Indus Valley civilisation, vanished without trace around 1700 BC. It was not until 1921 that archaeologists rediscovered the remains of this once-prosperous empire.

Sudden danger

Despite its rich soil, the Indus Valley was not an easy or comfortable place to live. There were swamps which harboured dangerous animals and disease-carrying insects. But a far more serious problem was that the river often flooded when it was swollen by monsoon rains. There was no way of knowing when these floods might happen, and when they did they caused huge damage.

After such catastrophes the Indus Valley people bravely repaired the damage, rebuilt their houses and carried on farming their fertile land. The river that sometimes seemed to be trying to destroy them also gave them food, water and wealth.

There was no shortage

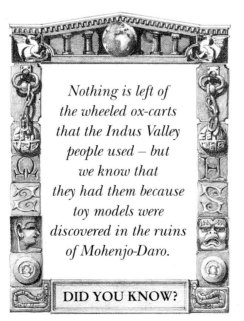

Nothing is left of the wheeled ox-carts that the Indus Valley people used – but we know that they had them because toy models were discovered in the ruins of Mohenjo-Daro.

DID YOU KNOW?

The great granary on the mound was where the wealth of Mohenjo-Daro was stored. At harvest-time, a continuous stream of ox-carts would deliver golden grain from the fertile fields along the Indus Valley.

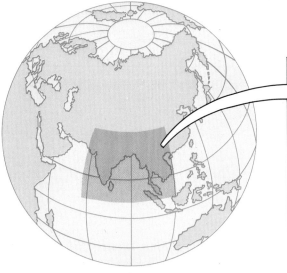

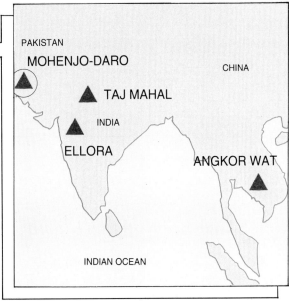

The site of Mohenjo-Daro today is about 400 kilometres (250 miles) from the Arabian Sea. But 4000 years ago it was nearer the coast, and small boats could easily reach the sea.

of building material in the Indus Valley. The mud of the delta could be baked to make bricks, or simply cut into shapes and left to dry in the sun. Mohenjo-Daro is a city of bricks.

City planning

Many ancient cities grew bit by bit, and this was probably how Mohenjo-Daro began. But the city the archaeologists found was carefully planned on a grid pattern, like a modern city. There was a broad main street crossed by many smaller streets, which in turn had narrow lanes leading off them. Many of the larger houses were built around courtyards with most of their windows facing inwards. This would have given security and kept the rooms cool.

The whole city had an efficient drainage system, with earthenware pipes carrying waste water from the houses to brick-built sewers beneath the streets. At regular intervals there were manhole-covers, which could be

removed so that the sewers could be cleaned. There are many cities in the world today that are less well organised.

The watchers on the citadel

The city was in two distinct parts. The houses were on the river plain, while to the west of them was a huge artificial mound, the citadel. A platform of mud bricks almost covered the mound, and the city's most important buildings – among them a massive grain-store and a large public bath-house – were built on it. The mound was overlooked by a number of brick watch-towers, as if it were a fortress.

If the mound was built for defence, who was the enemy? It seems likely that it was natural rather than human. The people of Mohenjo-Daro stored their grain well above water level to protect it from flood, and the watch-towers may have been intended to keep a check on the river. But this is only a guess. The purpose of the towers is one of many problems that we shall never solve for certain. Another is the question of what happened to the people of Mohenjo-Daro when disaster overtook them.

Decline and fall

Excavations have shown that the city was badly flooded many times and had to be partly rebuilt. It seems that, as the years went by, the quality of life began to decline. The later repairs were careless and some of the larger houses were divided into smaller units, suggesting there was an increasing population and a housing shortage. In its last days Mohenjo-Daro was no longer a splendid city but more like a slum.

By analysing soil samples, archaeologists have been able to build up a picture of what probably happened. Either before or after the city began to decay, disaster struck in the form of a severe flood caused by an earthquake. The drainage system would not have been able to cope with the rush of water, which would have run into the houses and damaged their foundations. Damage to the drains would have led to the spread of disease.

Meanwhile, the crops in the fields would have been ruined and the soil made useless until it could be drained.

A ghost city

After this disaster, the heart seems to have gone out of the people of Mohenjo-Daro. It was no longer possible to grow enough food for themselves, let alone enough to trade. Perhaps they fell back on the store in the granary until this stock also ran low. Perhaps they saw the end coming and gradually drifted away to try to rebuild their lives elsewhere. Whatever happened, by about 1700 BC the city was an empty shell.

Sacred animals

No temple has ever been found at Mohenjo-Daro, so we have no clear idea of what religion the people practised. But there are some clues.

Among these are stone seals that have been found at Mohenjo-Daro and at another Indus Valley site, Harappa. These were used to identify an individual merchant's goods for trading. Most of the seals are square, with a line of writing across the top and a carving, often of an animal, below. Unfortunately, the writing does not include enough different characters for archaeologists to be able to work out the language of the Indus Valley.

Animals that appear on the seals include tigers, rhinoceroses, crocodiles and elephants. But the animal that features most often is the Brahman bull with its hump, long horns and heavy fold of skin at the throat. The same breed of bull is held sacred by Hindu people today. Archaeologists believe that this suggests that the Indus Valley may have seen the start of Hinduism.

Seal showing a Brahman bull.

The citadel

Mohenjo-Daro was dominated by the great granary which stood on top of the citadel and was the city's most important building.

Measuring 45 x 23 metres (150 x 75 ft), the granary was built on a platform of brick and had tall, slightly inward-sloping walls and a brick subfloor. The grain would have been stored in wooden silos that sat on top of the subfloor. Inside, there were brick ventilation channels to allow air to circulate and prevent the grain from going mouldy.

The granary site was well organised for efficient working. There was plenty of space around it to allow ox-carts to come and go without hindrance. Along one side of the granary was a brick loading platform for the delivery and collection of grain.

The building with the courtyard beyond the granary in the picture was the great bath house. As well as a large, sunken pool about 2.5 metres (8 ft) deep, it contained several rooms with smaller private baths. Each of these rooms had a stone staircase leading to an upper floor.

Some archaeologists believe that the main temple of Mohenjo-Daro was also on the citadel mound, beneath the more recent Buddhist monastery that stands there now. However no trace of it has ever been found.

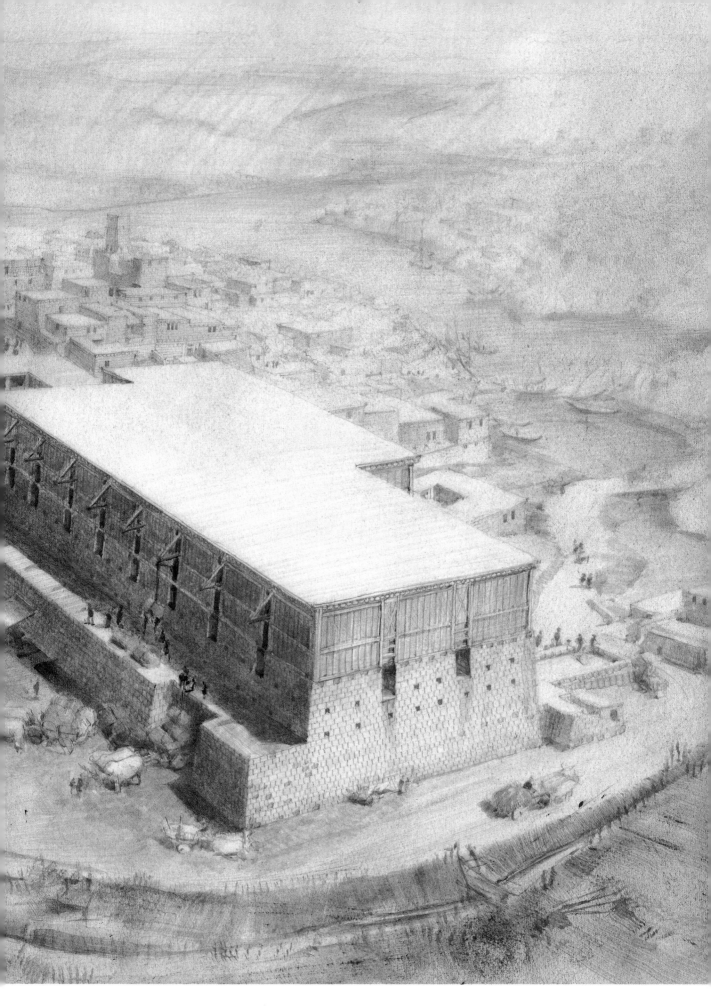

Cleanliness and godliness

The great bath-house on the citadel at Mohenjo-Daro is another clue that the religion of the Indus Valley people was in some ways like modern Hinduism.

The siting of the bath-house in such a prominent position suggests that it had a religious purpose. It seems likely that ritual bathing was a religious ceremony in the Indus Valley, just as it is among Hindus today. There were smaller private bathrooms off the main pool, which were probably used by the priests, who lived in the rooms above them.

A statue found at Mohenjo-Daro may show us what the priests looked like. It is about 18 centimetres (7 ins) high and shows a bearded man whose eyes are half-closed as if he is praying. His cloak is covered with a trefoil or clover-leaf pattern of a kind that is often found in religious sculpture in the remains of other ancient civilisations in Egypt and Mesopotamia (modern-day Iraq).

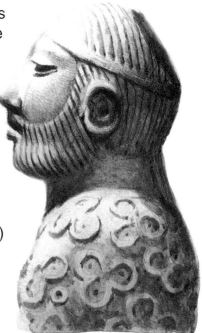

Statue of a priest.

The magic land?

The great wealth of Mohenjo-Daro came from trade. There is a structure in the city that looks like a dock and which would, before the later changes at the mouth of the Indus, have been beside the water. We know that boats from the Indus Valley civilisation crossed the Arabian Sea to the Persian Gulf because Indus Valley seals have been found at a number of sites there and even at Ur in Mesopotamia.

The Indus Valley may have been the magic land that was written about in Mesopotamia. This land, Dilmun, was in the east, where the sun rose. It was the source of luxury goods such as gold, silver, ivory and precious stones such as lapis lazuli, which were brought by ship to cities like Ur.

The people of Mesopotamia thought of Dilmun as a kind of paradise on earth. But whether Dilmun was the Indus Valley or not, there were certainly strong trading links between the two centres of civilisation.

A trading ship.

The power of water

As they flow from the mountains of Tibet through the foothills of the Himalayas, the waters of the Indus pick up and carry along a great deal of debris – sand, earth, and decaying vegetable matter. They are joined by tributaries which have also flowed from the mountains and brought debris down with them. When they reach the flat plain near the sea where Mohenjo-Daro stood, and the river flows more slowly, this material sinks to the river bed.

Over thousands of years, these deposits have filled up the river channels and forced the water to find new ways out to sea. At the same time, they have built up the land and pushed the coastline further out.

The result is that the course of the Indus as it approaches the sea has moved steadily westwards throughout history. Some of these changes will have happened gradually – but at other times, perhaps given an extra boost by storms or earthquakes, they took place suddenly and without warning.

It was these sudden changes that made Mohenjo-Daro so liable to flooding, and it was probably one particularly violent change in the course of the river that turned the city temporarily into an island which led to it being abandoned.

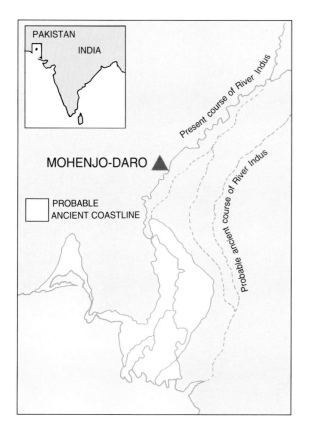

PAKISTAN
INDIA

Present course of River Indus

MOHENJO-DARO

Probable ancient course of River Indus

PROBABLE
ANCIENT COASTLINE

A lost civilisation

It was not until 1921 that modern archaeologists knew of the Indus Valley civilisation. In that year, the city of Harappa, which is much further up the Indus, was first excavated, and the next year work began at Mohenjo-Daro.

The major work at Mohenjo-Daro was led in the 1950s by the famous British archaeologist Sir Mortimer Wheeler. The great granary had already been excavated, but it was Sir Mortimer who realised what the purpose of this huge building had been. He also unearthed fortifications in the south-eastern corner of the city. He described his findings in two books published in the 1960s.

The Great Wall

China, c. 300 BC–AD 50

*Thousands of slaves, forced to work or die, built the Great Wall
to defend the China of the 'First Emperor'. Their work lasted longer.
He ruled for only eleven years, but the wall is still there.*

Along mountainsides, through deserts, over valleys and ravines, the Great Wall runs for 2400 kilometres (1500 miles) across northern China. When it was built, it turned the land to the south into a huge, securely-defended fortress. It is the largest single building project in the history of the world, and the only man-made object on earth which can be seen from the moon.

Rewriting history

Today, the wall is a world-famous tourist attraction, but it was built for a very different reason. Its main purpose was to defend China's cities and farmland from raiders from the north. Guarded by soldiers stationed in watch-towers like miniature castles, sited so that each could be seen from the next, the Great Wall was a constant warning to would-be invaders to keep out.

The Great Wall came to be built on the orders of one man who believed that he was the wisest and the greatest ruler in all history. To back his claim he had all earlier histories of the Chinese people destroyed.

The new empire

In 221 BC, after many wars between the rival families which ruled over separate Chinese states, Qin Shih-huang-ti became the first emperor of all China. He had many schemes for showing his own people and the raiders in the north that he was in complete control of his empire. Building the Great Wall was one of them.

He did not have to start from the beginning. Since about 300 BC the rulers of northern China had built lengths of wall along their borders. There were already about 2000 kilometres (1300 miles) of wall, mostly made of beaten earth and split up into separate lengths. Emperor Shih's

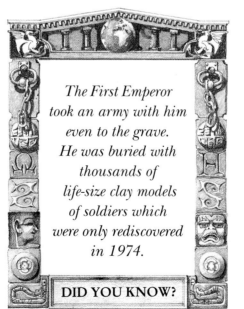

The First Emperor took an army with him even to the grave. He was buried with thousands of life-size clay models of soldiers which were only rediscovered in 1974.

DID YOU KNOW?

Foot soldiers of the Emperor's army wore lightweight armour so that they could move quickly. Perhaps this soldier is wishing he was back home with his family, working in the fields, and wondering if he will ever see them again.

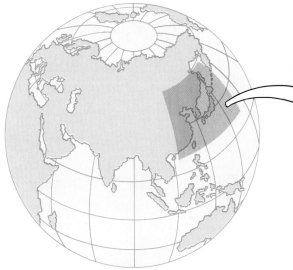

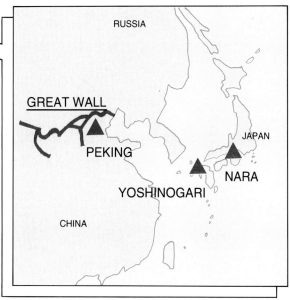

The Great Wall runs from near the coast of the Yellow River in the east to Yumen in the west, passing through some of the most hostile country in the world.

plan was to strengthen these and link them up, adding another 800 kilometres (500 miles) to make a complete line of defence to the north.

Prisoners in their own country
Although the wall's main purpose was to keep intruders out, it may also have helped to keep the Chinese people in. Many of them resented the harsh rule of Emperor Shih, and were tempted to move north to a greater freedom, including the freedom not to pay heavy taxes to the emperor.

Shih wanted all the Chinese people to be under his strict control, and the heavily-guarded wall would have been effective in stopping any would-be escapers from leaving. No one could enter or leave China without passing under the watchful eyes of the soldiers on the wall. The troops of the emperor's army did not take prisoners, and there was only one punishment for anyone they caught – death.

Record-breaking building project
Building the Great Wall was a huge task which was organised with military precision by one of the emperor's generals who was called Meng T'ien. It took twenty years to complete and over 300,000 slaves worked on it.

As the wall was being built in remote country where little food was grown, Meng T'ien's first job was to set up a chain of thirty-four supply bases for food and building materials. In some places there was no local stone and it had to be brought from great distances over specially-built roads.

From the start there was trouble with bandits who stole supplies and attacked the builders. It was necessary for soldiers to protect the workers, and before work started on the wall itself the watch-towers were built. These were at intervals about two arrow-shots apart, and they were large enough to house a garrison of soldiers, as well as give them protection. When the towers were complete, work began on the wall linking them together.

Worked to death
For the builders, forced to work on the wall away from their homes and families, conditions were terrible. Thousands were made to work so hard that they died. There were stories that the overseers of the work were viciously cruel, and that anyone who made a mistake would be killed and thrown into the wall's foundations.

Even without cruelty like this, things would have been bad. Working in mountainous country in all kinds of weather from burning sunshine to frost and snow, and in some areas in sandstorms, must have been exhausting.

To add to the workers' troubles, there was always the possibility of an attack by raiders, and food sometimes ran short when bandits held up supply wagons. Only strict military discipline could have kept the work-force together in such conditions. Many of the workers must have been tempted to make a run for it.

The land they left behind
The need for large numbers of workers on the wall and on Emperor Shih's other big building projects, and for foot soldiers for the army, caused problems for their families at home.

Most of China's 57 million people lived on the fertile land surrounding the Yellow River. Huge numbers of field workers were needed to cultivate the soil and produce enough food for the growing population. With so many men sent away to do building work or to join the army, it was difficult to farm, and this was another cause of the bitterness that led to trouble after Shih's death.

Muscle or magic?
Stories have been told about the Great Wall ever since it was built. Some Chinese thought that, as it twisted its way across the mountainous country of the north, it looked like a dragon. The image of a dragon was one that the Chinese were very fond of, and they turn up frequently in Chinese art and literature often symbolising the emperor.

Brick stamp with Chinese characters.

Another story tells how the Great Wall came to be built. Emperor Shih, it says, was a magician who created a flying horse.In one night he rode this wonderful animal right across China, and as he went, he mapped out the course the wall should take.

In another legend Emperor Shih is supposed to have owned a magic whip which he used to cut a way through the Daqing mountains in order to alter the course of the Yellow River so that the Wall could be built.

Action stations

Even in the large numbers shown here, raiders from the north would have been no match for the emperor's highly organised and well-equipped army.

Early warning of approaching enemies was given by sentries stationed on the watch-towers. There were thousands of these towers, about 12 metres (40 ft) high, giving a commanding view of the countryside from battlements, which also provided a safe base for archers. Today, only five towers remain.

The wall itself, about 9 metres (30 ft) high and 4.5 metres (15 ft) wide at the top, was enough of an obstacle to deter small groups of bandits. If there was a more serious threat, troops could move quickly and easily along the top of the wall to reinforce the guards in the watch-towers.

At intervals near the wall there were beacons for signalling, sited so that each could be seen from three others. A system of smoke signals was used to pass warnings along the wall about enemy movements, and to call up reinforcements. The only chance the raiders would have had of breaking through would have been a massive attack along the whole length of the wall – an impossible task.

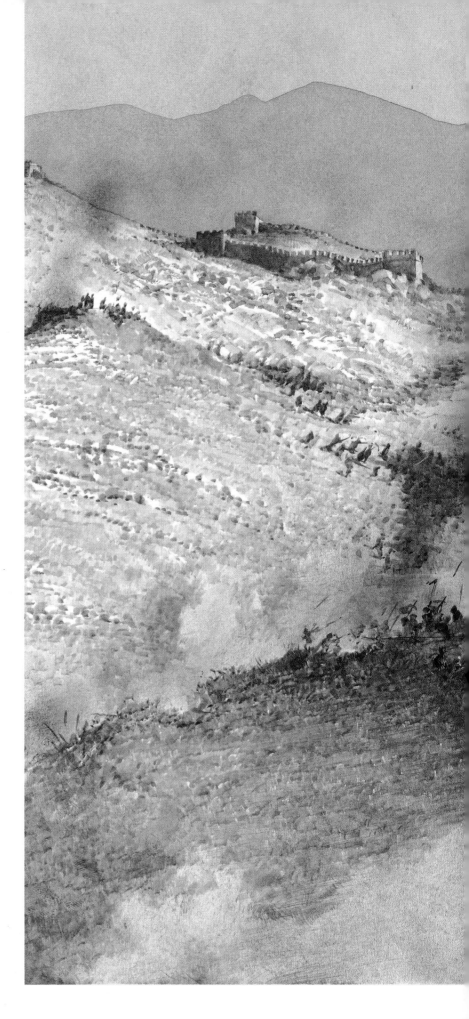

Raiders from the north

Who were the enemy against whom the Great Wall defended China?

The Chinese called them the Hsiung Nu. They were nomadic people, wandering with their herds of animals and carrying out raids on remote settlements in the north of China. If the Great Wall had not stopped them, they would have ventured further and further south until they were threatening larger towns and cities.

But not all the Chinese saw the Hsiung Nu as enemies. Some families, who had moved north to escape the emperor's rule, and had set up farms, were happy to trade with the nomads. This was a threat to the emperor's authority, and so the wall prevented trade as well as invasion.

There was a third reason for keeping a strong army in the north based on the Great Wall. Less than thirty years before Emperor Shih began ruling the whole of China, the last of the princes of the northern states had been defeated. There was always a risk of revolt against the new emperor's harsh rule, and that the rebels might gather round the leadership of one of the old princely families. It was important for the emperor to keep a tight hold on the border areas, because he had enemies not only beyond the Great Wall but also inside it.

Shih-huang-ti wanted to make sure that he would be safe from attack after his death as well. He ordered each province of the empire to make life-size, terra-cotta statues of the soldiers from that region and then to send them to where his tomb was being built on Mount Lishan in Shaanxi Province. Over 6000 of these statues, averaging 1.8 metres (5ft 9 ins) high and armed with spears, swords, bows and cross-bows, were buried in the huge mound raised over his grave. They were only rediscovered quite recently.

Life-size model soldiers from Shih-huang-ti's tomb.

Later history of the wall

In 210 BC, Emperor Shih fell ill and died, but the building of the wall went on. By AD 20 it was about 10,000 kilometres (6200 miles) long, completely sealing off the Chinese empire from Mongolia in the north.

After that, there was little new building, but the wall continued to be used and kept in good repair. As late as the sixteenth century AD, 9000 soldiers were stationed along it and 3000 new watch-towers were built. By this time the Great Wall was just part of a huge military complex, linking castles, garrison towns and fortified cities.

The First Emperor

Emperor Shih-huang-ti – the name means the 'First Emperor' – believed that his family, or dynasty, would rule China forever. He was wrong. Only three years after his death, rule passed to another family, the Han. But in eleven short years, Emperor Shih made China, which had been a collection of warring states, work as one country. His methods were ruthless; anyone who disobeyed his new laws faced death.

Several different languages were used in China. Emperor Shih decreed that there should be only one. He also laid down that only one system of weights, measures and coinage should be used, and even that carts should be only one size. New roads were built to link up the main cities of the empire, using slave labour, and marshes were drained to provide more farming land. For the Emperor himself a huge new palace was built.

All these changes were carried out with the help of the army. But when he died, it was the army that led the campaign to drive Emperor Shih's dynasty from power.

Shih-huang-ti.

The worst posting

Thousands of soldiers supervised the building of the Great Wall and manned it when it was finished. They did not choose to serve there. They were sent there on the orders of the Emperor.

Duty at the wall was unpopular. Many Chinese poems have survived, telling of the hardships soldiers had to endure. They were forced to spend years in the cold, hostile north, short of food and comforts, far away from their loved ones and ever on the alert for the approach of enemies.

Early Chinese money.

Tripod water pitcher.

Yoshinogari

Japan, c. 300 BC–AD 300

Yoshinogari is a place of unsolved mysteries. Who was buried in its great tomb? Why did thousands of people die in battle? Who were their enemies? So far, we can only guess at the answers.

Kyushu is the most southerly of the five main islands that make up Japan. There, only recently, Japanese archaeologists made one of their most interesting discoveries yet. When it has been fully explored, it may solve some of the mysteries of early Japanese history.

Giant grave mound

Yoshinogari was a settlement of thatched buildings surrounded by a moat. Although its first buildings may have been put up about 300 BC, it reached its peak around AD 300. The 600 years between these dates are called the Yayoi period of Japanese history. It was a time when rice-growing had become highly developed.

Several Yayoi settlements have been traced, but Yoshinogari is by far the biggest. It contains something that has been found nowhere else – a huge burial mound 24 metres (80 ft) long and 15 metres (50 ft) wide, standing on an even larger eight-sided platform. It is clear that someone of unusual importance was buried there. But who? We do not know – yet.

It may be that Yoshinogari was the capital and centre of Yayoi culture. Certainly it seems to have been a prosperous place. It was also the scene of a fierce and brutal battle.

Echoes of war

Among other things, Yoshinogari is a graveyard. As well as the great mound, several thousand graves have been found in which bodies were buried in clay urns. There were also 350 cave graves and more than ten graves made of stone. Only the bones are left, but they tell a chilling story. Some skeletons are without heads. Some have terrible wounds. Others have arrows stuck between their

The Japanese call their country Nippon. The name Japan used in the west came from the Chinese name Jih-pen, which means 'land of the sunrise'.

DID YOU KNOW?

About 300 BC, the Japanese began to develop new farming skills. They grew rice in paddy fields, and they tilled the better-drained land with ox-ploughs. The thatched buildings of Yoshinogari can be seen in the background.

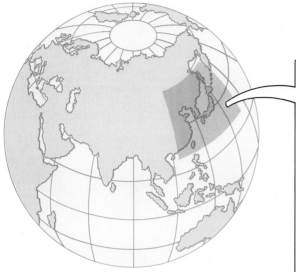

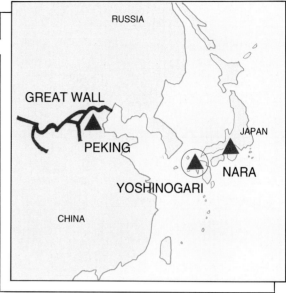

Yoshinogari is in north-west Kyushu, near the towns of Saga and Kurume and not far from Nagasaki. It was only a short way by sea from Korea, where there were Chinese colonies.

bones. What can have been the cause of all this pain and death?

In Yayoi times the islands of Japan were divided among a number of states which were at war with each other. There was also fighting between the people of the poor farming villages and the richer moated settlements. There may even have been fighting among the people of Yoshinogari itself, but the number of graves suggests something bigger than a local dispute.

Mirrors and mysteries

Apart from the graves, there have been many other finds at Yoshinogari which tell us about life in the settlement. These include many flat, crescent-shaped stone knives used for cutting rice. They have two holes through which a loop of string could be threaded. The string was wound round the fingers to form a handle.

There is also a good deal of decorated pottery and bronze

metalwork, crafts at which the Yayoi people were highly skilled. It is fairly easy to make small earthenware jars, but these people buried their dead in huge urns with lids, large enough to take a human body.

Many bronze mirrors, some small enough to be held in the palm of the hand and finely decorated with patterns, have been found. In the Yayoi period bronze mirrors were greatly valued as gifts and also had a religious meaning. But there were other, more mysterious, bronze objects. The discs with arms were particularly curious. It is hard to imagine what they might have been used for, but a large number have been found. There was even a stone mould for making them in large numbers, so they must have been of great importance, perhaps as jewellery.

The Land of Wa

Who were the people of Yoshinogari? Chinese travellers to Japan in the 250s

30

to 270s AD described a place which they called Yamatai, in the Land of Wa. They gave its position, measured by days at sea. However, the distance travelled at sea varies from day to day according to the wind and tide, so the Chinese measurements are not much use. None the less they could place Yamatai somewhere on Kyushu.

If this is the case, then Yoshinogari could be Yamatai, since it is the largest Yayoi site yet discovered. This would help to explain the huge burial mound as the grave of a king or queen of Wa.

Dances for the dead

If Yoshinogari really was Yamatai, we know something about life there from the stories brought back by Chinese travellers. The Yamatai people were said to be law-abiding, but there were harsh punishments for those who disobeyed the law. They had long lives, often surviving to be over 100 years old.

When they died, the ceremonies were long and followed strict rules. After burying their dead, the relatives mourned for ten days, while singers and dancers provided entertainment. At the end of the ten days everyone took a ritual bath in running water.

Rich and poor

The Chinese reported that there was a sharp division in Yamatai between the nobles and the ordinary people. When nobles approached, commoners had to get out of the way, and when speaking to nobles, they had to squat or kneel.

This seems to tie in with Yoshinogari, where the larger houses of the richer people – probably gathered round the royal palace which has not been found – were kept strictly separate.

Amaterasu, the sun goddess

The sun had an important place in Yayoi religion and culture, as it did in many other ancient civilisations.

Amaterasu, the sun goddess, was the chief of the Yayoi gods. Her great rival was Susanoo, the storm god, whose main aim in life was to cause trouble in the world.

One day, the legend said, Susanoo let horses loose in Amaterasu's rice fields, destroying her crops, and then damaged her palace. She was so upset that she hid in a cave, plunging the world into darkness.

Uzume, the goddess of fun.

To tempt her out again, Uzume, the goddess of fun, danced and sang and made such a noise that Amaterasu came out to see what was going on. At the entrance to the cave, the other gods had hung a mirror, the world's first. Amaterasu was fascinated by it and went closer to look at her reflection. Then the other gods grabbed her, dragged her out of the cave and the world was once more bathed in sunlight.

This story shows why the Yayoi people attached so much importance to mirrors.

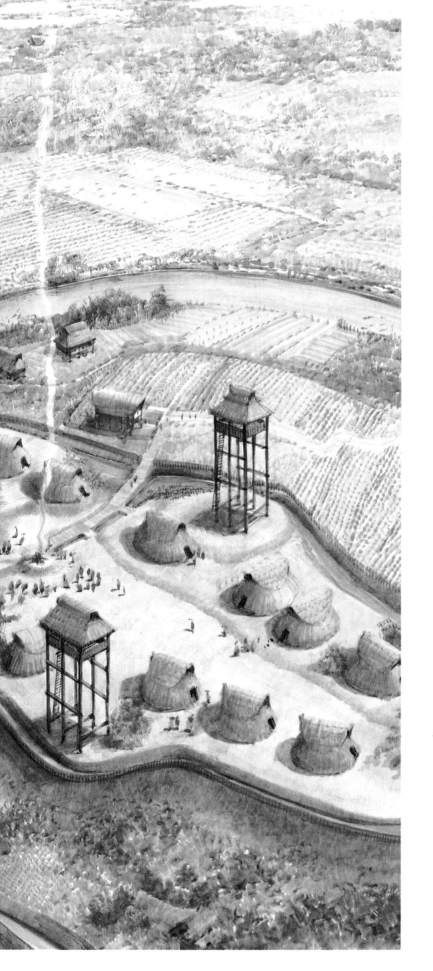

Yoshinogari, AD 300

This reconstruction shows Yoshinogari towards the end of its life. The outer moat surrounding the settlement was about 900 metres (3000 ft) long, and there was an inner moat to give added protection.

The oval or square houses were about 6 metres (20 ft) across, and were built of thatch over a wooden frame. The thatch came right down to the ground. In the middle of the floor of each house was a clay pit for a fire, and a bank of earth was built round the inside of the walls. This was used as a bench and for storage, and also stopped water from seeping into the house through the thatch.

Houses were not the only buildings in Yoshinogari. There were also grain stores, which were raised on wooden stilts to keep rats and other pests away.

Dotted around the edges of the settlement were tall watch-towers raised high on wooden frameworks. These gave a look-out from which approaching enemies could be spotted, and may have also been used to check that the people in the fields were working hard. Although Yoshinogari was a farming community, it was not a peaceful one, as the discovery of its grim burial grounds shows.

Queen Himiko

The great burial mound at Yoshinogari, larger than any other Yayoi grave yet discovered, poses a question. Who could have been important enough to be buried in such a huge grave?

Some Japanese archaeologists believe that it is the grave of Queen Himiko, queen of the Yamatai people for over sixty years.

Queen Himiko is said to have taken over Yamatai around AD 183 after a long period of war under a male ruler. Her name means 'daughter of the Sun'. Until recent times, emperors of Japan have claimed descent from the sun goddess Amaterasu. Himiko used magic and witchcraft to gain and keep power.

The female court

According to the Chinese, Queen Himiko ruled over the whole island of Kyushu, as well as part of neighbouring Honshu. She also built herself a heavily fortified palace. If the burial mound at Yoshinogari was hers, it is likely that her palace was also there, although so far its site has not been found.

To the Chinese, who were not used to the idea of a female ruler, all this seemed very strange, and they called Himiko's land the 'Queen Country'.

Chinese travellers reported that Queen Himiko lived in her fortress-like palace with 1000 female servants and just one man. He was not her husband. His job seems to have been to pass on her orders to the outside world.

The 'Queen Country'

To Chinese surprise, Himiko seems to have been a successful ruler. She encouraged trade and the exchange of visitors with China and Korea. Our knowledge of her comes from the Chinese visitors' reports of what they saw. But, as so often happens in history, her country soon began to fall apart after she died around AD 248. She was followed by a king, but he was unable to keep order. He was forced out of his palace, and a relative of Himiko, a thirteen-year-old girl called Iyo, was put in his place.

Clay head from a Yayoi tomb.

It is not certain what happened after that, but the great days of Yoshinogari were over. Perhaps the burial grounds of the victims of battle show how the settlement came to an end. Japanese archaeologists are still working on the site, and it may be that more and more of Yoshinogari's secrets will be revealed.

Queen Himiko and a Yayoi house.

Control of earth and water

Rice was the main crop of the Yayoi people. Their whole way of life depended on their skill in growing abundant crops by controlling the flow of water to the young rice plants. The same methods are used today in remote parts of Japan.

The rice fields were on slightly lower ground than that of Yoshinogari so that river water could flow into them. Earth banks divided the paddy fields and helped to control the flow of water. They also provided paths for workers on their way to the fields.

It is important to control the water supply throughout the growing period of rice plants. So there would have been ditches or canals between the fields to allow them to be irrigated or drained.

Rice was not the only crop grown by the Yayoi. Where the land was dry enough, ox-drawn ploughs were used to cultivate the soil to grow millet, a kind of corn. The Chinese also reported that farmers in the Queen Country grew melons, a variety of vegetables, and planted mulberry trees to feed their silkworms.

Storage jar.
Right: Woman's head in clay from a burial chamber.

Chinese travellers' tales

Almost everything we know about the Queen Country and what life might have been like in Yoshinogari, apart from archaeological finds, comes from two Chinese writers who visited Japan about 250 years apart.

The first writer went to Japan around AD 57 and described what he found. At that time, the Land of Wa was ruled by a king. Then, around AD 297 the *Wei Chih*, the history of the Wei dynasty, was written. Some of the information in it was taken from the earlier book, but it also describes Queen Himiko, her way of life, and her burial.

The *Wei Chih* is not an account of one person's travels. It is a collection of reports from travellers at different times over at least 250 years and maybe more. Some of it is probably gossip that was passed on from one person to another before it was written down. As a result we cannot take everything in the *Wei Chih* as fact.

Ellora

India, c. AD 600–900

*Among fast-running streams and plunging waterfalls, the
thirty-four temples at Ellora are set like jewels on a hillside, with intricate carvings
and gigantic statues inviting worshippers of three religions.*

The thirty-four temples at Ellora would be a sight worth seeing even if they had been built in the usual way. There are huge statues standing in high, vaulted halls, while sculptured wall panels tell stories of the gods. There are pillars, staircases, life-size stone elephants and lions, gate-houses guarding the shrines and bridges linking them. The thirty-four temples of Ellora run for 2 kilometres (1.25 miles) along a cliff face among the mountains of Hyderabad in western central India.

However, the most remarkable thing about Ellora is that its temples were not built stone by stone – they were carved out of the solid rock. They are man-made caves, one of which is over 30 metres (100 ft) long. Another way of thinking of them is as gigantic sculptures.

Living in harmony
Three of India's great religions have temples at Ellora. Twelve were made by Buddhists, seventeen by Hindus and five by Jains. In turn, they tell the story of how religious belief was changing in India over about 300 years.

Although they are different in so many ways, Buddhism, Hinduism and Jainism all attach great importance to quietly searching for truth. The cool, dark temples of Ellora, almost cut off in the mountains, were perfect places for followers of all three religions to shut themselves away from the world.

Buddhist monks were the first to come to Ellora around AD 600. Some of their temples were plain rooms hollowed out of the rock, surrounded by smaller cells where the monks could go to pray and study on their own.

There were also monasteries where they could live and eat. These had a large central hall, with stone tables for meals and a shrine with

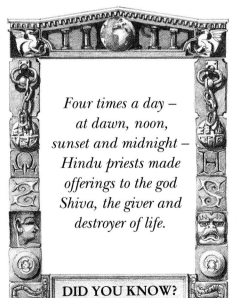

Four times a day – at dawn, noon, sunset and midnight – Hindu priests made offerings to the god Shiva, the giver and destroyer of life.

DID YOU KNOW?

*The Kailasanatha is the most spectacular of Ellora's temples. Here, a bird's eye view
of the temple is superimposed on a plan showing the roof's supporting pillars. Above are two of the
figures from Hindu legend which decorate the walls.*

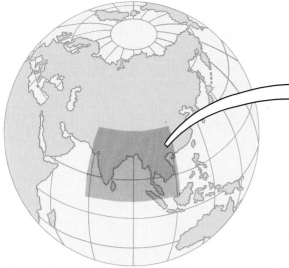

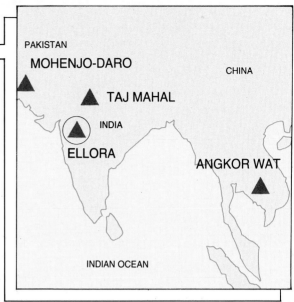

Ellora is in the state of Maharastra in western central India. It was on the major trading routes, which would also have been followed by pilgrims to Ellora's shrines.

a statue of the Buddha at one end. The monks slept and studied in small cells round the walls.

Watched by the Buddha

The temples known as Cave 10 and Cave 12 seem to have been the most important Buddhist sites. They were carved around AD 700 and are more magnificent than the others.

In the central hall of Cave 10 a huge figure of the Buddha sits on a stupa, or throne, whose top reaches almost to the ceiling. This ceiling has been carved to resemble wooden rafters, and other details suggest that the builders' aim was to recreate the feel of worshipping in a wooden temple.

Cave 12 is arranged in three storeys. The lowest one contains the entrance and a hall decorated with sculptured wall panels. There is another large hall, over 30 metres (100 ft) long, on the second floor, but the top floor is the most magnificently decorated. There,

another large hall, its roof supported by forty-two pillars, is watched over by statues of the Buddha on stately thrones, attended by other Buddhist saints who look on from wall panels.

Temple of victory

The Buddhists were still putting the finishing touches to Cave 12 when Hindus began to carve out their first temples at Ellora. The most spectacular Hindu temple is the Kailasanatha. This was begun in AD 765 on the orders of King Krishna I, who ruled north-western India. It was his way of giving thanks to the Hindu god Shiva for victories in battle.

In fact, the Kailasanatha is not one temple, but a whole group of temples standing in a deep pit. Its construction was a huge undertaking. Working from above, the builders cut trenches 30 metres (100 ft) deep in the solid rock. Then they drove tree trunks into the trenches and poured in water. The water made the wood swell, and this pressure cracked the rock.

When the loose rock had been dug out, a solid piece of rock 85 x 49 metres (280 x 160 ft) was left. It was from this that the Kailasanatha was painstakingly carved, using only chisels about 2.5 centimetres (1 in) wide. The same simple tools were used to carve the sculptures that decorate most of the temple's outside and inside walls.

Past the sacred bull

The sides of the pit, connected to the Kailasanatha by bridges, have shrines cut into the rock from which visitors can see the sculptures on the outside walls. Inside there are gateways, galleries, staircases and shrines.

Visitors enter the temple through the shrine of Nandi, the sacred Brahmin bull, which is guarded by two life-size stone elephants. Beyond this is a bridge which leads to the main hall of the temple. This has sixteen columns and measures about 16 metres (43 ft) square. Beyond that is an inner shrine where only the priest was allowed to go. Smaller shrines surround the main hall.

The god of war

Of the five Jain temples, the Indra Sabha is the one most admired by visitors. It was carved around 850. This too was cut out of the rock from above, and is rather like a miniature Kailasanatha. It is decorated with patterned pillars, carved entrances and sculptured wall panels showing Indra, the god of war. A huge lotus flower is carved in the ceiling.

At Ellora followers of each religion found ways of expressing their beliefs in stone as solid as their faith.

Lord of the dance

Shiva – the god to whom the Kailasanatha was dedicated – is one of the three main Hindu gods. Hindus believe that he is the creator and destroyer of all things. He can give life or take it away. He is lord of the beasts, the protector of cattle, the great god of death and the lord of time.

In Hindu temples Shiva is shown in many different ways. Sometimes he is seen riding his sacred bull Nandi. He is also often shown as the lord of the dance, as in this eleventh century bronze image.

In Hindu legend, Shiva's dance is called the tandava. It begins slowly, but becomes more and more wild and fills the whole universe with its excitement. Shiva dances so furiously that he threatens the universe with destruction.

In this bronze Shiva is dancing on the body of Forgetfulness. This was a reminder to Hindus that although Shiva created life he can also destroy it.

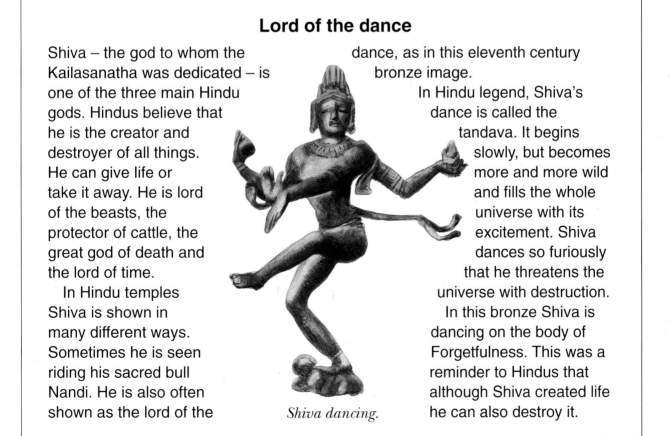

Shiva dancing.

The religions of India

Three of the six main religions in India today – Buddhism, Hinduism and Jainism – are represented at Ellora. The absentees are Islam, Sikhism and Christianity; none of them appeared in India until after the Ellora temples had been carved.

Three lives

Hinduism grew out of the beliefs and legends of India itself and those of the Aryan people who invaded India about 3500 years ago. Unlike most other religions, it does not have a fixed set of rules laid down by a leader such as Islam's Mohammed or Christianity's Jesus Christ.

Hindus believe that everyone has three lives – past, present and future. If you are a Hindu, your place in this life depends on how you behaved in your past life. How you behave in your present life will decide what happens to you in your future life. If you behave very badly, your next life may be as an insect or an animal.

There are many Hindu gods. Some of them are worshipped by individual families or by single villages, but there are three main gods. We have already met Shiva, the giver and destroyer of life, on page 39. The others are Brahma and Vishnu. These three all have families of lower gods to help them carry out their work.

Brahma was the creator of the world. His lower gods look after the Sun, Moon and stars and keep them all in their places. Vishnu rules the world. His lower gods control the weather, among other things. All other Hindu gods are related in some way to these three.

The great teacher

Buddhists think of their leader, the Buddha, as more of a teacher than a god. The word Buddha means 'one who has found the truth'.

The real Buddha was a prince called Gautama Siddhartha, who was born into a Hindu family about 2500 years ago in what is now Nepal. He was brought up in his father's palace, protected from all knowledge of the outside world. When he was sixteen he married a princess, Yasodhara, and they had a son.

Now that he had a household of his own, the Buddha could go wherever he wanted. This was how he discovered how much suffering there was in the world. He was so shocked that he left his family and spent many years wandering through the countryside, trying to work out why so many people had such unhappy lives.

One day, as he sat under a wild fig tree, the truth came to him. The sufferings of this world did not matter. One day, everyone would find escape from the cycle of reincarnation that the Hindus believed in by achieving nirvana, or total happiness and peace. This was to be done by understanding

Figure from the temple facade.

that existence is unhappiness and the way to escape existence is by destroying your selfish desires. He spent the rest of his life teaching what he had discovered.

Gods in human form

Budddhists believe that, when someone achieves nirvana, his or her spirit merges with the universal life of the world. However, some good men and women who have achieved nirvana decide to remain as divine beings in the world to help men and women to salvation.

Respect for life

The Jains broke away from the Hindus around 300 BC and took on some of the ideas of Buddhism. They follow a very strict diet, and one of their central beliefs is that no living thing – not even the smallest insect – should be killed.

Buddha.

The colonnade surrounding the Kailasanatha.

Rediscovering Ellora

The temples of Ellora were never 'lost' through floods, buried by earthquakes or destroyed by war. They have been there, for anyone to see, ever since they were carved, but they were unknown outside India until, in 1794, they were described by a British traveller, Sir Charles Ware Malet.

His account aroused the interest of other people interested in India's history, but it was not until 1824 that anyone realised that the temples, which were rapidly becoming ruins, should be preserved.

A British army officer, Captain J. B. Seely, recognised the importance of Ellora, and began a campaign to save the temples. He was successful, and it is thanks to his efforts that we are able today to admire the work of the skilled Indian masons of over 1000 years ago.

The *Mahabharata*

Witchcraft, magic, miracles, monsters, demons and gods all have a part to play in the *Mahabharata*, one of the great collections of Hindu myths. It tells the story of a great battle between two families for the throne of the Kuru kingdom in north-western India.

A family quarrel

The two families were the Pandavas and the Kauravas. There were five Pandava princes, whose father King Pandu died while they were still children. There were 100 Kaurava princes, who were cousins of the Pandavas. In the *Mahabharata*, the Pandavas represent good and the Kauravas evil.

When the cousins grew up, they quarrelled over who should be King of the Kurus. The Pandavas thought it should be the eldest of the five brothers, Yudhisthira. The Kauravas put forward their eldest prince, Duryodhana.

They decided to settle the matter over a game of dice – but Duryodhana cheated and won. However, he agreed that if the five Pandava brothers would leave the country for thirteen years Duryodhana would hand over the throne of the Kurus when they returned. But of course Duryodhana had no intention of keeping his promise.

So for thirteen years the Pandava brothers roamed about the world and had many adventures, including some narrow escapes from death. Once, the Kauravas arranged for a house where they were staying to be burned, but the Pandavas heard of the plot just in time. Another time, they met a man-eating demon. One of the Pandava brothers, Arjuna, met a beautiful princess who gave him the power of becoming invisible in water, and from the god Shiva himself he received a magic weapon.

The great battle

At the end of thirteen years, the Pandava princes returned to claim the throne. Duryodhana refused to give it up, so the Pandavas had no choice but to try to win it in battle. Both sides gathered their forces and met on the plain of Kurukshetra. The God Krishna had befriended the Pandavas, so he fought on their side.

The two armies lined up facing each other. There were archers in chariots, swordsmen on horseback, lancers mounted on elephants, and thousands of foot-soldiers armed with bows, swords and javelins. The battle raged for eighteen days, until at last the five Pandava brothers were the only princes left alive.

Then Yudhisthira, the eldest, was crowned King of the Kurus. He reigned for many years with the help of his brothers, the *Mahabharata* says, and brought peace and wisdom to his people.

Krishna was also a wonderful flute player.

The *Ramayana*

Another famous collection of Hindu stories is found in the *Ramayana*. It tells how Prince Rama fought and killed Ravana, the King of Sri Lanka.

Ravana was a fearsome creature. He was a demon with ten heads and immense strength. He had so pleased the gods by his prayers and self-discipline that they promised that no god or demon could kill him. But then he caused so much trouble that the gods decided to get rid of him.

The kidnapped princess

The gods agreed that the only way to kill Ravana was for one of them to come to earth as a human. They had not promised that Ravana could not be killed by a man, and he had been too proud to ask for this protection.

So it was decided that the god Vishnu would be reborn as a human baby, and when he grew up, he would kill Ravana. Accordingly, Vishnu was reborn on earth as Rama and Vishnu's wife Lakshmi was reborn as a princess called Sita. When they grew up, Rama and Sita were married.

But Ravana was jealous of Rama and wanted the beautiful Sita for himself. He tricked Rama into going hunting, and while Sita was alone Ravana captured her and took her away to Sri Lanka in his flying chariot.

Rama gathered together an army and set out to rescue his wife. He chose as his general Hanuman, the god-king of the monkeys, whose magic powers included the ability to fly.

They came to the narrow sea that divides India from Sri Lanka. Hanuman flew on ahead and told Sita that Rama was on his way to rescue her.

Hanuman, armed for battle.

Meanwhile, Rama had ordered the sea to part so that his army could march across, but nothing happened. When Hanuman returned, he showed his monkeys how to build a bridge, and five days later this was ready for Rama's army to cross.

Rama's triumph

There was a great battle outside Ravana's palace. At first, things went badly for Rama and he was wounded. But Hanuman knew of a magic herb that would cure him, and flew all the way to the Himalayas to fetch it.

Then Rama and Ravana were left alone to fight it out. Rama took aim and, one by one, shot off Ravana's ten heads – but they grew again. So Rama shot again, this time using a magic arrow. This passed through Ravana's body and killed him.

Rama and Sita returned home, where Rama reigned for 10,000 years before being taken up into the sky and resuming his position as Vishnu.

Nara

Japan, c. AD 710–95

*It was a perfect city. The people there dressed in the finest silks,
dwelt in beautiful houses and spent their lives in leisure and luxury.
Only the best was good enough for the people of Nara.*

One day in AD 645 there was a sensation at the Japanese imperial court. The empress's brother, her son and a courtier burst into the palace, threatened the empress and killed her chief adviser. This man belonged to the Soga family who had been the power behind the Japanese throne for many years. Prince Naka, the empress's son, himself dealt the fatal blow.

Japan would never be the same again.

Eager to learn

There had been many changes in Japan in the three hundred years since Yoshinogari was abandoned (see page 29). It was only a short distance by sea from Korea to the most southern Japanese islands, and Chinese ideas and culture had easily crossed the narrow straits. Chinese civilisation was more advanced, and the Japanese were eager to learn all they could from it. In AD 405 Japan adopted the Chinese system of writing in picture-characters.

In 552 the religion of China, Buddhism, was introduced in Japan. The imperial family became Buddhists and encouraged the building of Buddhist temples. From around 600 there were regular visits to China by Japanese monks, scholars and officials, who spread the ideas they brought back.

Steadily, Japan came to resemble a miniature version of the Chinese empire, with the same system of government and similar laws. But meanwhile, the Soga family had become so powerful that they seemed poised to take over the throne. That was why Prince Naka and his fellow plotters decided that the power of the Soga must end.

Power behind the throne

Prince Naka allowed his mother to continue to

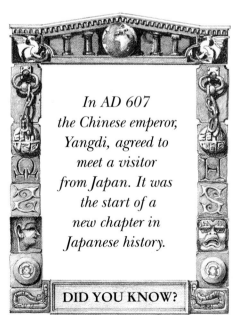

In AD 607 the Chinese emperor, Yangdi, agreed to meet a visitor from Japan. It was the start of a new chapter in Japanese history.

DID YOU KNOW?

*A man and woman of the imperial court at Nara.
Courtiers had ample spare time in which to admire nature, read and write poetry,
enjoy music and take part in graceful court ceremonies.*

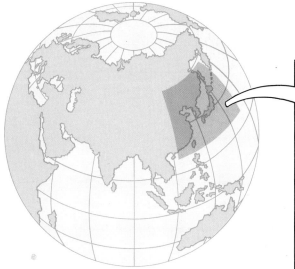

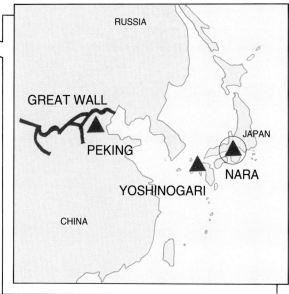

Nara, in the south of the main Japanese island of Honshu, is close to the modern city of the same name. The imperial family chose a completely new site for its new capital.

reign as empress, but from then on he was Japan's real ruler. When his mother died in 661, he became emperor and took the name Tenchi.

However, he had already begun a programme of change for Japan. He took power away from the noble families. He made new laws about the collection of taxes and the ownership of land. And as a sign that Japan was breaking away from its past, he began to make plans for a new capital city, Nara.

A perfect city

As it turned out, Emperor Tenchi did not live to see the new city built. It was his successor, the Empress Gemmei, who gave the order for building to begin. But Tenchi chose the site and helped to plan it. Although work did not begin until 708, Nara was the city that Tenchi had dreamed of.

Nara was designed as the control centre from which Japan would in future be governed. Empress Gemmei's orders were that it should be planned as a complete and perfect city. Nothing should have to be added later.

So, from the start, Nara had everything. Carefully planned and laid out on a grid plan, it had palaces, offices for tax-collectors and other government servants, markets, granaries, Buddhist monasteries and pagodas. Its buildings and streets were beautifully proportioned. Its palaces and great houses were wonderfully furnished. It was a city of dreams.

A life of luxury

For the rich and powerful families who lived in Nara, life was very pleasant indeed. They furnished their homes, and dressed themselves, with the finest silks and brocades. They filled their houses with beautifully made, inlaid and lacquered furniture and objects made of tortoiseshell, ivory and mother of pearl. Visitors to China had described the palaces of the Chinese emperors, and

Empress Gemmei was determined that hers should be just as luxurious.

Life at court was one of leisure and luxury. The imperial family and their courtiers enjoyed music, poetry, art and the study of nature. They had endless supplies of money to spend on whatever they liked. Where did this wealth come from? The answer was: from the poor.

Rich and poor

If you let a jug of milk stand for a while, the cream rises to the top. There is only a small amount of cream compared with the mass of milk. The Japanese society that supported Nara was rather like that.

The cream at the top represented the rich, powerful families who lived in Nara. They were supported by the much larger number of poor families who toiled in the fields, producing rice or other grain or tending the silkworms which spun the silk for the clothes and homes of the rich.

Time for change

Out of their earnings, the poor had to pay heavy taxes. The harder they worked, and the more they produced, the more they had to pay in tax. They paid for the leisured lives of the privileged people of Nara, but they did not share in it.

In the end, this unfairness finished Nara. Around 794 many poor families abandoned their fields in a protest against the imperial taxes. The Buddhist monks took over this land and so increased their power.

It was time for another change, and the then emperor, who was called Kanmu, ended Nara's (and the monks') power by moving the capital to another city, Kyoto. Nara's dream was over.

An earthquake-proof building

A pagoda is a tower, usually five storeys high, with the roof of each storey overhanging the lower one. Each storey is smaller than the one below.

The ground floor of a pagoda is a Buddhist shrine where people can come and worship. The upper floors, reached by spiral staircases, are for prayer, for quiet thought, or simply for people to admire the view.

The pagoda is another idea that Japan borrowed from China, but it was particularly useful in Japan, which is in one of the world's major earthquake zones. Pagodas are built round a central wooden post, which supports the rest of the structure.

The Japanese found that, as all the stresses of a pagoda were concentrated on its supporting post, it was better able to withstand earth tremors than other types of building. This discovery explains why pagodas became such a feature of Japanese architecture. They pleased the eye, and they also had real practical value.

A pagoda in a garden.

The Horyu-ji monastery in about 710

Among all the magnificent buildings of Nara, the most splendid were its Buddhist temples and monasteries. The Buddhist belief that the miseries of this life must be endured for the sake of a better life after death suited a system that demanded hard work for little reward from most people. The period when Nara was built was the peak of Buddhism in Japan.

The oldest surviving Buddhist monastery of

the time is the Horyu-ji which lies about 18 kilometres (11 miles) from Nara. There was an even earlier monastery on the site before Nara became the imperial capital, but it was destroyed by fire in 670 and rebuilt about twenty years later. The monastery that stands on the site today is the oldest wooden building in the world.

You enter Horyu-ji through a two-storey gateway, a kind of shortened pagoda. Inside is a

courtyard with two buildings in the middle. These are a pagoda and the two-storeyed main hall known as the Kondo. Beyond the main courtyard are the monastery's other buildings, including a library and rooms for monks, students and visitors.

Although the wood of which the monastery was built has, of course, been renewed over the centuries, Horyu-ji still looks much the same as it did nearly 1500 years ago. Buildings of stone or brick would not have survived Japan's earthquakes, but wood, which moves in response to earth tremors, is more durable.

The monasteries inside Nara itself were even more magnificent than Horyu-ji. Successive emperors tried to outdo each other in building even more splendid temples to the Buddha, thereby gaining merit for their piety.

The Great Buddha

In the temple at the centre of the monastery stands the Great Buddha of Todai-ji, 16 metres (52 ft) tall. The Buddha is not alone. He is attended by two statues of Bodhisattvas (see page 43).

At the corners of the temple stand statues of the Four Great Kings who, in Buddhist legend, guard the north, south, east and west. Each is about 13 metres (43 ft) high.

In another hall there are yet more statues of the 'guardians' of Buddhist legend. One, Fukukensaku Kannon, wears a silver crown inlaid with pearls, quartz and agate. Another, Shukongo-jin, carries a thunderbolt to set on anyone who threatens the Buddha.

A Bodhisattva.

Shomu's temple

Around 735, Japan was struck by an outbreak of smallpox, which was then a fatal disease. The story goes that the then emperor of Japan, who was called Shomu, had a number of his relatives who died in this epidemic.

Either in the hope of preventing more deaths, or perhaps in thanksgiving once the outbreak was over, Shomu ordered a huge statue of Buddha to be made, with a new temple to house it. The result was Todai-ji, the finest of all Nara's monasteries.

One of the Four Great Kings who guard the Todai-ji.

Centre of power

In 741 Emperor Shomu ordered that Buddhism should have a central base of power, and the Todai-ji was chosen as the national temple. Emperor Temmu had earlier, in 685, commanded that every house in the land should have a Buddhist altar.

The emperors and the Buddhist monks made a concerted drive to install Buddhism as the national religion of Japan. After 741 the monks controlled worship of the Buddha from there through branch temples in every part of the country.

A national poetry collection

With plenty of time on their hands, the courtiers of Nara gave some of it to the arts, and the Nara period saw the beginning of Japanese literature. The first national histories were written, together with an account of the different provinces of Japan. But the greatest work of literature, and one that gives us a picture of how the Japanese of the time thought and felt, was the *Man'yoshu*.

The *Man'yoshu* was a collection of about 4500 poems by many different writers. Some were written by members of the imperial family, and some by monks or courtiers, but others were the work of ordinary people.

One poem, for example, was about the sadness of a frontier guard, longing for the girl-friend he left behind at home and wishing she were the bow that he carried with him on duty. Others, written by monks, told of their unhappy lives of poverty.

But many poems in the *Man'yoshu* were celebrations of the beauties of nature. The poets wrote about the countryside, plum and cherry blossom and the wonders of snow, moonlight and running water.

Interestingly, few of the poems are about Buddhism and they show little sign of Chinese influences. It may be that in their writing the poets were saying what they really felt about life, and not what they were told to feel by the emperor.

A courtier reading poetry.

The greedy monks

The devotion of the Japanese imperial family to Buddhism gave an enormous amount of power to the monks and priests. One of the first to realise this was Ganjin, a famous Chinese monk who arrived at Nara in 753. Soon, he was teaching in the imperial court and was given a palace of his own which he turned into a monastery.

This was only the start. Before long, monks were suggesting all kinds of extravagant building projects to the imperial family and their courtiers. Monks planned the buildings and suggested what precious objects should be placed in them. They designed rich robes for themselves to wear. The emperor would pay – but of course the money really came from the ordinary people who had to put up with higher and higher taxes.

Towards the end of the Nara period, the monks also became involved in government. Their influence and power grew and grew. At last, Emperor Kanmu decided that this must stop. In about 794 he moved the imperial capital away from Nara to Kyoto and ended the power of the Nara monks. They had become too greedy.

Angkor

Khampuchea, c. AD 900–1150

*For five centuries the Khmer empire was the major power in what we now call
Indo-China. Its kings built more than 900 temples.
Angkor Wat – both temple and royal tomb – was the greatest of them.*

The Mekong, one of Asia's longest rivers, flows for 4500 kilometres (2800 miles) southwards from the mountains of China to the South China Sea. Its waters, as they near the sea, spread out to make a fertile flood plain. It was here that one of Asia's lost empires, the kingdom of the Khmer, began to flourish about 1500 years ago.

Traders and farmers

The rich crops of rice grown on the plain of the Mekong were the original source of Khmer wealth, but the people also became skilled in metal-working and in carving objects in ivory and coral. They built up strong trading links with India and China.

By about AD 800 the Khmer King Jayavarman II had set up his capital at Angkor. It was to be the first of many cities built on the same site. But it was not until about 1150, in the reign of King Suryavarman II, that the Khmer people achieved their greatest work with the building of the vast temple of Angkor Wat.

Breathtaking beauty

Angkor Wat stands on an island about 800 metres (880 yd) square, circled by a wide moat 200 metres (650 ft) across. It is reached by a single causeway across the moat, skilfully placed so that the approaching visitor can appreciate the full beauty of the building.

The effect is made even more breathtaking by the reflection of the temple's terraces and towers in the water of the moat. Inside, there are ornamental pools sited to catch the reflection of the towers again and to throw light upwards on to the stonework. Whoever designed the beauties of Angkor Wat was someone of great skill and sensitivity.

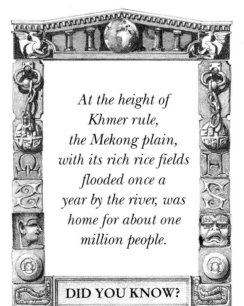

At the height of Khmer rule, the Mekong plain, with its rich rice fields flooded once a year by the river, was home for about one million people.

DID YOU KNOW?

*While the god-king sleeps, a young girl entertains his spirit with
a traditional dance. Dancing was a frequent theme of the sculptures at Angkor Wat
and the other temples of the Khmer empire.*

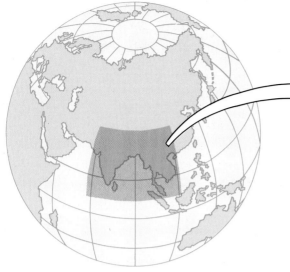

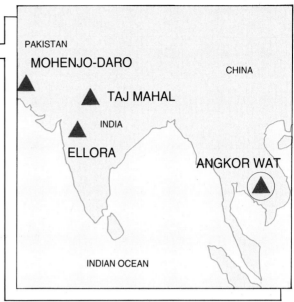

The several cities of Angkor were on the northern slopes overlooking the Great Lake of Khampuchea (or Cambodia). Water from this lake flows into the River Mekong.

The mystery of Angkor

For many years after its discovery in 1860, archaeologists puzzled over Angkor Wat. It seemed to be partly a Hindu and partly a Buddhist temple, and yet it contained other features that seemed to belong to neither religion. We know now that the Khmer religion took in ideas from both Hinduism and Buddhism – and also that the Khmer people worshipped their kings as gods.

During King Suryavarman II's lifetime Angkor Wat was used as a temple. When he died, it became his tomb. Although the temple's carvings and statues celebrated heroes from the Hindu *Mahabharata* and *Ramayana* (see pages 40–4), they had a second meaning. They were tributes to the heroic and wise rule of the king who would one day be buried there.

For both Hindus and Buddhists, the centre of the universe was Mount Meru, with its five peaks. This idea is copied in the large courtyard at the centre of Angkor Wat. Pyramid-shaped towers stand at each corner of the courtyard, and in the centre is the Great Pyramid, the temple-mountain and royal tomb.

Star-shaped spires

One of the reasons why Angkor Wat stands out among the buildings of the world's ancient civilisations is the Khmers' unusual designs and building methods. The towers stand on square bases, but as they rise through nine levels of stonework they become star-shaped, tapering towards the top.

The Khmers used no mortar to hold the stonework in place. Each level of stonework is linked with iron bars driven into the stone, but otherwise the masonry is held together only by weight and gravity. What is perhaps even more surprising is that the temple has almost no foundations. But the structure was so carefully planned that it has remained standing in almost perfect condition for nearly a thousand years.

The Khmers at war

We know little about King Suryavarman II, except that he was responsible for the building of Angkor Wat and died around 1150. His reign of about 37 years saw the Khmer empire reach its peak.

After his death, there was war between the Khmer and the rival kingdom of Champa to the east, in what is now Vietnam. In 1177 the Khmer capital of Angkor, about 1.6 kilometres (1 mile) north of Angkor Wat, was attacked by Champa soldiers and left partly in ruins.

Four years later, a newly-crowned king, Jayavarman VII, set about rebuilding his capital and avenging the Champa attack. The new capital was Angkor Thom, a walled city about 3.2 kilometres (2 miles) square with five monumental gates. It included another great temple, Bayon, rivalling Angkor Wat in size and beauty.

The end of an empire

However, Jayavarman VII was too ambitious. He began a military campaign aimed at taking over the whole of south-east Asia from Myanmar to Vietnam, plus the Malay peninsula.

The Khmer empire did not have enough people to man a huge army as well as carry out the king's building plans and continue the everyday work of farming. Jayavarman VII could not hold on to the land he had fought to win, and his control even over the Khmer land began to fall apart.

The Khmer empire staggered on, steadily becoming poorer and weaker, for another two hundred years. Eventually, in 1437, Angkor fell to the Thai army and much of the city was destroyed. Over the next hundred years, the Thais gradually gained control over the whole Khmer empire, whose glories were forgotten for more than three hundred years.

The kingdom of Funan

Before the growth of the Khmer empire, its territory was occupied by the kingdom of Funan. This came into being around AD 50 and was the major power in Indo-China for about five hundred years.

The entrance to Angkor Wat.

A legend about the foundation of the kingdom of Funan tells of an Indian sailor and explorer called Kaundinya who travelled eastwards until he came to Indo-China. There, he met a native princess who was half human and half serpent. They married, and together ruled over the region.

It may be that there really was a leader who had come from India and married into the ruling family. It is certain that links between Funan and India were strong, and that the people of Funan were once Hindus. The Khmer people at that time lived in what is now northern Khampuchea under Funan rule. Around 550 they ousted the Funan king and took control for themselves.

Towering achievement

Angkor Wat was designed so that visitors, approaching the temple along the causeway across the moat, are led from one exciting view to the next.

Visitors enters through the great doorway on the right in the reconstruction below. Beyond, there is a huge gallery decorated with stories from Hindu legends carved in the stone walls. A series of staircases then leads them slowly

upwards to the outer courtyard of the temple, guarded by towers at the corners.

The inside walls of this courtyard have galleries and are decorated with more legendary figures. More steps lead up to the central courtyard. Again, there are towers at the four corners, but here, in the centre, is the focal point of the whole temple – the huge central tower built for the king.

With its many staircases, terraces, galleries and courtyards, Angkor Wat offers the visitor a succession of different views of its central temple. These views are multiplied again by the reflections in the ornamental ponds and moat. None of these effects is accidental. They were all carefully planned so that the last resting-place of King Suryavarman II would be a place of continuing pleasure and wonder to his people.

There is no great hall at Angkor Wat where the people could gather for worship as the temple was first and foremost the home of their god-king. The priests would have carried out ceremonies in the many side-temples, but people would have visited Angkor Wat partly to admire its beauty, partly to enjoy the stories retold in its carved wall-panels, and partly as pilgrims.

The god-kings of Khmer

A carving of Suryavarman II as a god-king.

How did worship of the Hindu and Buddhist gods become entangled with the worship of the Khmer king as a god himself?

The answer may be on the island of Java, now part of Indonesia, over 1600 kilometres (1000 miles) to the south. As a young man King Jayavarman II had lived in Java as a prisoner of its king. There, the king was regarded as a god, and Jayavarman may have brought this idea back with him when, about 790, he returned to his country to take power among the Khmer. The Khmer already accepted many Hindu and Buddhist ideas side by side, so the idea of a god-king was easily added to the mixture.

By the time Angkor Wat was built, about 1150, the idea of a god-king had become thoroughly absorbed into Khmer religion. The figure of Suryavarman II is brought into many of the carved retellings of Hindu myths,

and there is even a pair of wall panels showing members of the Khmer court taking part in a procession to heaven and hell.

Probably Suryavarman's courtiers took the hint that his friends would end up in heaven and his enemies in hell. To be sent to the Buddhist hell was a terrible sentence. No soul sent there was released for at least 500 hell years – and each day of a hell year equalled fifty years on earth. So the Khmer courtiers would have taken care, if they were wise, to stay friends with the king.

Health and wealth

There were other reasons why Jayavarman II may have seemed like a god to his people. His predecessor had been a weak ruler who had wasted away the wealth of the Khmer empire. Under Jayavarman, the empire's fortunes revived. He was an enthusiastic builder, not only of temples but also of canals for both transport and irrigation of the land. The Khmer became prosperous again.

What is more, Jayavarman II reigned for sixty years. Towards the end of that time it must have begun to seem to his people that, like the gods, he was immortal.

A detail of one of the causeway statues.

Stories in stone

Angkor Wat is full of sculpture. There are long sequences of pictures from Hindu legends, carvings of demons and gods, dragons and other mythical creatures, and real-life animals such as lions, snakes and monkeys. Among all these pictures are panels which illustrate everyday scenes of Khmer life, such as fishermen at work.

One spectacular series of carvings tells the story from the *Ramayama* of the great battle between Rama and Ravana outside the gates of Ravana's palace in Sri Lanka.

Another series takes its subject from the *Mahabharata*. It shows the battle of Kurukshetra, when the armies of the Pandavas and the Kauravas fought it out for the leadership of the Kurus. (You will find both these stories in the chapter on Ellora.)

There is only one reason why a king should order that stories of the people's heroes be retold on the walls of his personal temple. Suryavarman II wanted his people to think of him as another hero in the same tradition and as a great and good king. He wanted to be remembered when he died as having the same courage, the same wisdom and the same immortality as the heroes of old.

Khmer fishermen casting their nets.

Lost in the jungle

After Angkor declined, it lay forgotten and gradually became completely overgrown with jungle vegetation. It was not until 1860 that a French naturalist, Henri Mouhot, came upon the ruins by accident as he was collecting plant specimens in the jungle.

The discovery changed Henri Mouhot's life, for from then on he became an archaeologist. He made the first accurate plans and sketches of Angkor and was the first to bring news of its wonders back to Europe.

Until the 1950s, Indo-China was a French colony, and Henri Mouhot's work was followed up by later French archaeologists who cleared and restored Angkor Wat and the neighbouring temple of Bayon, built a century later.

Easter Island

Oceania, c. AD 1100–1680

On a tiny island far out in the Pacific Ocean,
people lived until 250 years ago as they had lived since the Stone Age.
But how did they come to settle in such an isolated spot?

On a map of the world Easter Island is a tiny speck in the middle of the Pacific Ocean. It is only about 25 kilometres (16 miles) long, and its nearest island neighbour is over 2000 kilometres (1200 miles) away. Apart from its isolation, it is one of the last places in the world that anyone would choose to live. It is a barren, rocky place with hardly any trees.

Yet this tiny island at one time supported a population of several thousand people. Where did they come from, and how did they get there? These are only two of the mysteries of Easter Island.

The most famous feature of Easter Island is another of its mysteries. This is the collection of 600 huge statues, some finished and placed in position and others half-completed, with which the island is dotted. With only stone tools, and with no wheeled transport to carry the statues into position, how did the islanders manage such a massive undertaking?

Lost continent

Ever since European sailors came across Easter Island more than 250 years ago, there have been many theories about where the Easter Islanders came from and how they got there. Some of these theories were very imaginative. At one time it was even suggested that Easter Island was all that was left of a continent that sank into the ocean, leaving only a few survivors.

Archaeologists now agree that the first people on Easter Island travelled there from somewhere else. But did they come upon it by accident, perhaps after a shipwreck? Or was their voyage planned? And where did they start from?

Thanks to scientific methods of dating, we have a fairly accurate idea of when the first settlers arrived. It was

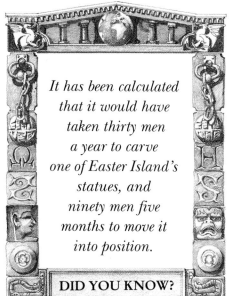

It has been calculated that it would have taken thirty men a year to carve one of Easter Island's statues, and ninety men five months to move it into position.

DID YOU KNOW?

The huge statues of Easter Island were probably raised using ramps and levers, with the red stone topknots lashed into place. A modern experiment showed that a team of twelve men could raise a statue in this way in eighteen days.

Far away from any of the Pacific's shipping lanes, Easter Island was taken over by Chile in 1888. Its only contacts with the outside world are a weekly plane and an occasional Chilean ship.

around AD 400, but there is no firm evidence about where they came from. It must have been either the islands of Polynesia, nearly 2000 kilometres (1200 miles) away to the west, or the mainland of South America – an even more challenging voyage of around 4000 kilometres (2485 miles) to the east.

Heroic voyage

The explorer Thor Heyerdahl with his Kon Tiki expedition (see pages 63 and 67) proved that a voyage from South America would have been possible, given the skills of the South American people. But this did not prove that such a voyage had actually taken place.

Other archaeologists say that the culture of Easter Island is closer to that of the Pacific islands to the west than to that of South America. The move to Easter Island, they say, was more probably part of a general movement of people to the east from south-east Asia. This view is generally accepted nowadays.

Whoever is right, the voyage to Easter Island must have been one of the great journeys in the history of the world, calling for immense courage. The settlers would have been aboard tiny boats – probably outrigger canoes – with only limited supplies of food and water. They would have had no way of knowing how far they had to go or how long it would take. That they found Easter Island at all is almost a miracle.

Stone Age people

Once they arrived, the settlers soon began to make the most of their new home. Their skills and tools were those of the Stone Age. They fished with hooks made from stone or bone, ate from stone bowls, used stone axes and made knives out of volcanic rock. They had no pottery or metal tools.

Archaeologists divide the history of Easter Island into three stages. The first stage, which they call the Early Period, lasted from about 400 to 1100. During this time, the Easter Islanders began to build terraces or platforms, usually facing the sunrise. They may have been sun-worshippers. Some statues were also carved at this time, but not the famous large ones.

These came later, in the Middle Period between 1100 and 1680. More platforms, called ahu, were built, and the enormous statues, mostly between 3–6 metres (10–20 ft) tall, placed on them. These statues, with their long heads and long ears, have a strong family resemblance. They were carved from carefully selected volcanic rock, yellow-grey for the bodies and red for their topknots.

Volcano workshop

The statues were carved out of solid rock in a quarry on top of an extinct volcano in the east of the island. They were almost finished when the islanders took them to a lower working site where the last touches were added. Meanwhile, the red topknots were being cut from stone in another quarry to the west.

We do not know how the islanders transported statues weighing many tons to their chosen sites. They had no wheeled transport, so they probably used some kind of sled. Another mystery is how the statues were raised into position. The painting on page 60 suggests one possible method.

The final realistic touch was probably added when the statues were in place. This was to give the heads eyes, using coral for the whites and red rock for the irises.

A name for every head

Carving the statues, then transporting and erecting them must have occupied an enormous amount of time, and it is surprising that the Easter Islanders, struggling to survive in a fairly hostile environment, could spare it. It is clear that the statues meant a great deal to them. The islanders told early European visitors that each statue had a name, and it is likely that each was put up as a memorial to a dead king or chief.

After around 1680, in the island's Later Period, statue-building came to an end. Maybe the population shrank, and perhaps time could no longer be spared. It also seems likely that there was an outbreak of fighting. The islanders' stone houses fell into ruins and the people took to living in caves or rough shelters. The great days of Easter Island were over.

Thor Heyerdahl

Born in 1914, Thor Heyerdahl is a Norwegian explorer and anthropologist who became fascinated with the question of where the Easter Islanders came from. In 1947 he sailed from Peru in South America to Easter Island on the Kon-Tiki raft (see page 67) to show that this voyage would have been possible. He believes that there have been two separate cultures on Easter Island. The statue-builders, he says, came from South America and were only followed much later, after 1680, by settlers from the east. However, other archaeologists dispute this claim.

Heyerdahl returned to Easter Island in 1955 to lead the first thorough investigation of its mysteries. He was particularly interested in the remains of the stone houses on the island. These date from the Middle Period, before the islanders took to the caves and other shelters.

As there are few trees on Easter Island but no shortage of stone – and the islanders were skilled masons – it was natural that they should build their homes of stone. These homes had low walls about 1 metre (3 ft) high, with a steeply-sloping roof of thatch. This was cut away at one point to allow for a full-length door.

Although doubts have been cast on Thor Heyerdahl's theory of a Pacific crossing from the west, his work on the island revealed a great deal of new and valuable information about Easter Island's Middle Period.

War on Easter Island

Was there ever a war on Easter Island? Stories told by the islanders suggest that there was. It seems to have taken place during the seventeenth century, and perhaps it marked the division between the island's prosperous Middle Period and the poorer Late Period.

Long Ears and Short Ears

The islanders said that there were battles between two sides called the 'Long Ears' and the 'Short Ears'. The Long Ears, who had red hair and white skin, had ruled over the Short Ears and had organised the carving and erection of the statues. Eventually the Short Ears rebelled against the Long Ears' demands.

There had been fighting and the Short Ears besieged the Long Ears on a peninsula of the island, which was defended by a ditch filled with brushwood. However, the Short Ears managed to scale the cliffs and attacked the Long Ears from behind. They drove them back against the ditch which other Short Ears had set alight and most of the Long Ears men were killed.

In the course of these battles, some of the statues were pushed over and the terraces where they stood were used as burial grounds for the casualties of the war.

Who were these two opposing sides? It is not hard to imagine that on a small island where there were few resources and farming land was scarce, disputes could have broken out between rival families. Again, perhaps the islanders who worked on the statues wanted to spend their time on more productive work on the land.

A third possibility is that the war was between the older settlers and new arrivals. This would fit in with Thor Heyerdahl's idea that a new group of people from the east came to the island around 1680. And, as the eighteenth century explorer Captain Cook reported, there were two distinct groups of islanders, some small and dark and others larger, with light skins and red hair.

One chapter in Easter Island's history is, sadly, not a myth. In the nineteenth century Peruvian slavers arrived on the island and kidnapped around 1000 of its people to work in the mines. Many of them died on the journey, and only five or six survived to return to their remote home.

Stone sculptures from a secret cave on Easter Island.

Rongo-rongo

Among the many mysteries of Easter Island are a number of wooden tablets discovered there in the nineteenth century.

The tablets have inscribed on them what is obviously writing. But the language, which has been given the name Rongo-rongo, is unknown, and the only people who were able to read them were among the slaves shipped off to Peru.

There have been many guesses at the purpose of the tablets. One idea is that they contain details of the ceremonies followed in Easter Island's Late Period by the island's priests, who were called rongo-rongo men. One tablet seems to be a summary or index to all the rest. But it is surprising that the people of Easter Island, for whom mere survival can never have been easy, developed a written language in addition to their other achievements.

The islanders' spoken language, unlike any other that the first explorers had ever heard, was equally difficult to work out. It is sad that the rapid decline of the island's culture soon after the first Europeans arrived, followed by the capture of so many islanders as slaves, means that much of what the people of Easter Island could have passed on about their history and their lives will now always remain a mystery.

Part of a rongo-rongo tablet.

Captain James Cook

The first Europeans to land on Easter Island were a party of Dutch sailors who arrived on Easter Sunday 1722, and so gave the island its name. But it was the British sailor Captain James Cook who brought back to Europe the first detailed description and sketches.

Captain Cook led three expeditions to the Pacific with the aim of finding the 'great southern continent' which was supposed to be there. On the second, in 1773, he called at Easter Island, which he knew about from the reports of the earlier Dutch visitors.

Despite problems with the language, Cook did his best to find out what he could about the statues, which at that time were still standing upright. By the time the next visitors arrived, they had been toppled and left face downwards. Captain Cook was killed in Hawaii on his third expedition in 1779.

Bird worship

All over the world, people look out for the arrival and departure of migrating birds as a sign that the seasons and the weather are changing. In an isolated spot like Easter Island, such signs of the natural calendar may have been especially important, showing that it was time to plant seeds or that shoals of fish, such as tunny, were about to return to the waters around the island.

This may explain why, in the south of Easter Island, a religion seems to have built up surrounding the annual visits of the migrating sooty tern. The sooty tern is known for its graceful flight and is sometimes called the sea swallow. Like other members of the tern family, it migrates huge distances. In spring flocks of sooty terns land on Easter Island to lay their eggs.

A sooty tern in flight.

The village of Orongo at the south-western tip of Easter Island was a group of forty-eight stone huts built sometime around 1500. A short distance off the shore was a small island called Moto Nui. On the rocks of the coast nearby are many carvings of men with birds' heads, some carrying eggs. Quite clearly, the birds had some unusual meaning in the lives of the people of Orongo.

The great egg chase

There may be a link between the bird-carvings and a story told by some of the older people of Easter Island about an annual competition, or perhaps a religious ceremony, involving the eggs of the sooty tern.

Every year, it seems, the heads of the leading families would gather at Orongo at about the time when the sooty terns were expected to arrive. Each family would send a servant to swim across to the island of Moto Nui to wait for the terns to arrive and start nesting. The first servant to find an egg would swim back to Orongo with it, and his master would receive special honours for the rest of the year.

Bird ceremonies may have been brought to Easter Island by visitors or settlers from the east. In the book he wrote about the Kon-Tiki expedition Thor Heyerdahl described a bird dance he saw performed on Raroia, an island about 3800 kilometres (2400 miles) to the west of Easter Island. He described this as 'one of the oldest ceremonies on Raroia', and it seems to have been a dance of welcome.

It may be that the Easter Islanders took the idea of welcoming the migrating sooty terns, which heralded the coming of spring and built their own ceremonies round it.

The Kon-Tiki expedition

Thor Heyerdahl's interest in Easter Island began by comparing stories told by old people in the islands of the South Seas with those of the people of Peru. One figure cropped up in both sets of stories – the sun god Tiki. Could the Tiki of the South Sea Islands and the Tiki of Peru be the same god? And if they were, did that mean that there had been a migration of people from South America half-way across the Pacific?

The idea teased at Thor Heyerdahl's mind for many years until, in 1946, he began to plan a voyage which would test his theory. He designed a raft made of trunks of balsa wood of the kind used by the ancient Peruvians, tied together with hemp ropes, and with a square sail. He added deck planks and a cabin made of bamboo. He also found a five-man crew and a parrot prepared to undertake the hazardous journey.

Many people begged him to call the whole thing off because it was so dangerous, but he persisted, allowing only a few precautions such as four months' supply of food, a two-way radio, and a rubber dinghy for emergencies. Finally, on 28 April 1947, the Kon-Tiki expedition set out from Calleo harbour in Peru.

It was a voyage of adventure and sometimes of terror. At times the *Kon-Tiki* was becalmed. At others, it was tossed about in a raging sea. The crew fed themselves mainly from what they could catch from the sea, using both fish-hooks and a fine nylon net for plankton. They also fished for sharks which would approach the raft, in Thor Heyerdahl's words, 'like hungry dogs'.

At last, after a voyage of 102 days covering about 6500 kilometres (4060 miles), the raft made its landfall on Raroia Islands reef, this is about 800 kilometres (500 miles) west of Tahiti. The raft was wrecked on the coral reef as they tried to get ashore, but survived as did everyone on board.

As Thor Heyerdahl later wrote, the Kon-Tiki expedition did not prove his idea about people sailing from South America to the islands of the Pacific was right, but it proved that such a voyage was possible. Before *Kon-Tiki* no one would have believed that six men on a frail balsa-wood raft could possibly survive such a journey in dangerous and lonely waters. Thor Heyerdahl did not solve the mystery of Easter Island, but his expeditions raised some fascinating possibilities.

The Kon-Tiki *raft under sail.*

Great Zimbabwe

Zimbabwe, c. AD 1200–1450

*Once believed to be the site of the legendary King Solomon's mines,
Great Zimbabwe proved to hold even greater secrets
which have not yet been disclosed.*

Between the two great rivers of East Africa, the Zambesi and the Limpopo, a high plateau rises to 1200 metres (4000 ft) above sea level. Here, about a thousand years ago, an area where people had for centuries made a poor living from the land became a prosperous kingdom with trade links stretching far beyond Africa. This was the kingdom of the Shona people, and its main city was Great Zimbabwe.

Today Great Zimbabwe is an irregular honeycomb of stone walls dominated by a large egg-shaped enclosure called the Elliptical Building. The oval is 100 metres (300 ft) across at its widest point, and it has a double wall over 9 metres (30 feet) high. The whole site covers an area of nearly 40 hectares (100 acres).

Kingdom of gold

The discovery of the ruins of Great Zimbabwe in the mid-nineteenth century caused great excitement. There were age-old stories of a kingdom in the centre of Africa which had supplied the gold used in the fabulous palace of King Solomon described in the Bible. There was gold in the hills to the north of the settlement, and various gold trinkets were found among the ruins. Could this be the site of 'King Solomon's mines'?

Explorers who hoped to find treasure at Great Zimbabwe were disappointed. But investigations showed that it had once been a thriving trading community and the most important of the one hundred or so settlements in the area.

The first settlers in the area arrived around AD 300. They grew grain, raised livestock and used iron tools. Their homes were built of daga, a mixture of clay and gravel. They seem to have been peaceful people, quietly getting on with their lives and

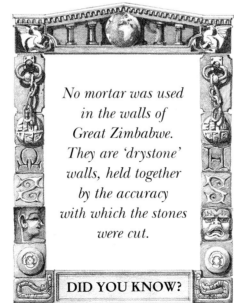

No mortar was used in the walls of Great Zimbabwe. They are 'drystone' walls, held together by the accuracy with which the stones were cut.

DID YOU KNOW?

Venturing inland in search of goods to trade, Arab merchants mixed with Shona traders in the markets of Great Zimbabwe, exchanging beads and cowrie shells for gold and ivory. Alongside them, local people bartered grain and meat for pots and ornaments.

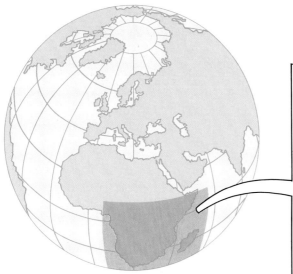

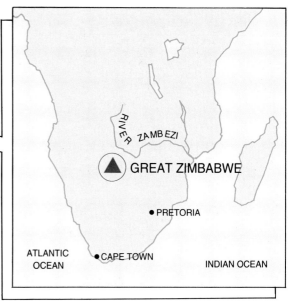

Great Zimbabwe is about 150 miles (240 kilometres) north of the Limpopo River. Before Zimbabwe became independent in 1980, it was called Rhodesia.

not bothering much about the world beyond the plateau.

Ambitious newcomers

In about 900 new settlers arrived. Perhaps they were members of an expanding tribe which needed more land. They were more ambitious than the original Great Zimbabweans. They extended the farming land, built up herds of cattle, mined for gold and began to build in stone. They were also more interested in the outside world as a source of trade. These were the founders of the settlement whose ruins survive today.

Trade brought wealth, and wealth produced a gap between rich and poor. The rich emerged as leaders of the community, and by about 1300 the people of Great Zimbabwe – the Shona – had a king. The Elliptical Building enclosed his palace and was probably also the centre from which trading was organised.

Home-making

The Shona people continued to build their homes of daga, giving the walls a finishing coat of smoothed clay. Their huts were circular, about 3–6 metres (10–20 ft) across, with smooth clay floors and framed wooden doors. They were roofed with timber and thatch, which was supported on wooden poles around the outside walls. Most huts had one or two rooms, with daga platforms to sleep on.

The Elliptical Building also contained daga buildings, probably larger than the other huts. Sections of the inside were partitioned off with stone walls, and to one side there was a solid stone, cone-shaped tower about 9 metres (30 ft) high. In front of the tower was a large, stepped platform, perhaps used for some kind of religious ceremony. Other daga platforms had statues on them.

The Shona people learned their skills as stonemasons as they went along. Their earlier walls were crudely made and uneven. Later, blocks of even shape and size were used. This was just one of the crafts at which the Shona became expert.

Expert craftspeople

There was a flourishing iron industry in Great Zimbabwe. Arrowheads, spearheads, knife blades, axe-heads and hoes have all been found, together with ironworkers' tools such as tongs for handling red-hot metal, hammers for beating it into shape and wire-making tools. As well as iron, the Shona also worked in gold, copper and bronze, from which they made bracelets, anklets and other ornaments.

They were also skilled potters, though they had no potters' wheels and used the more primitive 'coil pot' method. This involved rolling out a long 'sausage' of clay and then coiling it into shape, the edges of the coils being smoothed together. This technique made useful small pots for their own use, but they would not have been good enough to trade. There was already a brisk trade from abroad in far better pottery made on a wheel.

Spinning and weaving were also practised, possibly using cotton. But the heart of the community, and the reason for its success, was farming. Shona farmers produced large amounts of grain. They also tended large herds of cattle, which they moved from the plateau to lower ground according to the season.

Rituals of Great Zimbabwe

There are no written accounts of life in the Shona kingdom at this time. We have to base our idea of what it was like from the objects left behind and from what we know of the later lives of the Shona people.

Early explorers found, scattered about Great Zimbabwe, stone columns about 1 metre (3 ft) tall. Some of these had been topped with carvings of birds in grey-green soapstone. The columns were found mounted on the outer walls, and also in groups on daga platforms.

We can only guess at the meaning of these columns and the strange bird carvings, but there are two clues. Later Shona people worshipped the spirits of their ancestors, and some central African peoples still use similarly shaped objects to represent their ancestors in religious ceremonies. It may be that the Great Zimbabweans behaved in a similar way.

The conical tower inside the Elliptical Building may also have had a religious purpose. It has been suggested that its shape is like that of the bins which, until recently, were used in the area to store grain. The platform in front of it may have been the scene of a religious ceremony, perhaps at harvest-time when the grain was gathered in.

A soapstone bird statue.

A mud-walled city

Both the daga huts and the stone walls of Great Zimbabwe were unusual in avoiding right-angled corners. The huts were circular, while the walls that divided groups of huts were less regular in shape, but curved gently when they changed direction.

This reconstruction shows Great Zimbabwe as it was about 1300, at the height of its power and importance. It has been estimated that at this time there were between 100 and 200 adults living in the settlement. Most of them would have been craftspeople or traders. Another 1000 to 2500 people lived in the other smaller settlements on the plateau, working as farmers or herdsmen.

The illustration shows clearly how the Elliptical Building, with its conical tower in the foreground, dominated Great Zimbabwe. It shows, too, the Elliptical Building's strange double wall. Was this built to defend the ruler and his family inside? Or was it to make the Elliptical Building stand out as the most important enclosure in the settlement? Certainly the double wall seems to have been built with the greatest care, and it is decorated with a zigzag pattern along the top, which may have had some special meaning.

Trading ventures

From about 800, Arab traders, sailing down the Red Sea and southwards along the coast, began to build up links with East Africa. They set up trading ports on the coast and built up a thriving business in the export of timber, iron, ivory, horn, gold and, later, slaves. As trade grew, they travelled further into the interior in search of goods to exchange. The variety of objects from abroad found at Great Zimbabwe suggests that the settlement lay on one of the trading routes used by the Arabs. Some were luxury goods such as pottery from Persia (now Iran) and China, where the craft was much more advanced than in Great Zimbabwe. But there were also more everyday things, such as glass beads, brass wire and cowrie shells.

In exchange for these novelties, the Shona people had two valuable and much-prized things to offer – ivory and gold.

Ming dynasty flask from China; this sort of china was found at Great Zimbabwe.

Death of a city

Great Zimbabwe was at the peak of its prosperity between about 1200 and 1450. Then, quite suddenly, it was abandoned. What went wrong?

At about the same time, there was an important change in trading down the coast of East Africa. The Portuguese arrived, driving out the Arab merchants and taking control for themselves. Of all the things that East Africa could offer, the Portuguese were most interested in gold. But this should have helped Great Zimbabwe, not destroyed it. There was gold nearby, and good profits could have been made from trading in it.

Yet this did not happen. It seems likely that, just before the Portuguese arrived, some great disaster fell upon Great Zimbabwe. It may be that the land was simply exhausted by continuous farming over the centuries and unable any longer to provide enough food. Or it may be that the cattle herds were infected by disease, perhaps carried by the tse-tse fly. There may have been a drought. Whatever the reason, it seems that the population shrank quickly, and that those who were left moved on to settle elsewhere. Some time soon after 1500 Great Zimbabwe died.

A tse-tse fly.

Archaeological prejudice

When archaeologists first discovered Great Zimbabwe in the 1860s, they were amazed to find that such a well-developed civilisation could have existed in what they thought of, in those days, as a continent inhabited by 'savages'. Africans, they said, could not have built the Elliptical Building or the network of stone walls around it.

Phantom Arabs

This raised a question. If Africans did not build Great Zimbabwe, who did? The nineteenth-century archaeologists chose the Arabs. Some linked the story of 'King Solomon's mines' with Great Zimbabwe and suggested that Arabs had built the settlement to exploit the gold that lay nearby. Others had the idea that Arabs from northern Africa had travelled south and founded the community.

Nineteenth-century Europeans grew up

The Great Tower.

with the idea that civilisation began in the Middle East and spread to Europe. It did not occur to them that peoples in other parts of the world might have made their own discoveries of the uses of iron, how to build in stone, and the other skills of early cultures. Great Zimbabwe upset their fixed ideas about world history, and they did not like having to think it all out again.

Sheer greed

European narrow-mindedness explains some of the wilder theories about Great Zimbabwe. Others are explained by sheer greed. People convinced by the 'King Solomon's mines' theory launched themselves into a great treasure hunt, finding little but doing lasting damage to the site. It would have been better if Great Zimbabwe had been left undiscovered until less prejudiced archaeologists turned up.

The truth about Great Zimbabwe

Early in the twentieth century, a new generation of archaeologists studied Great Zimbabwe and did so with less prejudiced eyes. Among them were David Randall-MacIver and Gertrude Caton-Thompson.

They came with open minds and accepted that Great Zimbabwe was part of Africa's own culture. They placed the settlement as having been built between AD 1100 and 1300, and not in Old Testament Biblical times. In other words, Great Zimbabwe belonged to Africans, and not to outsiders. More recent investigations, using scientific dating methods, have confirmed this.

The Forbidden City

Beijing, China, c. AD 1404–50

The Chinese empire of the Ming dynasty was huge, powerful and rich.
The centre of its power was the Forbidden City,
open only to people who had been invited by the emperor.

First came twenty-four drummers, followed by twenty-four trumpeters. One hundred armed guards were next, with one hundred mace-bearers. Four hundred attendants carried torches. There were lancers, fan-bearers and officials. Finally, there was a great chariot drawn by an elephant.

The Ming emperor of China was making one of his rare excursions outside the Forbidden City of Peking, as Beijing was then known.

through a series of further gates: the Gate of Heavenly Peace, the Meridian Gate, the Gate of Supreme Harmony and the Gate of Heavenly Purity. These led through the Tartar City to the Imperial City and then to the Forbidden City, the home of the emperor and the centre of the Chinese empire. However few visitors could go this far. The Forbidden City was so called because only people favoured by the emperor were allowed inside.

Inside four walls

The Forbidden City itself was just as splendid as the emperor's procession. It was the innermost of four walled cities that made up the capital of China.

The outermost area was called the Chinese City. Through the great gate in its northern wall, the Qian Men (or the Imperial Way) led to the inner cities.

The visitor passed

From the Forbidden City Emperor Yong Le ruled over 100 million people in the largest empire the world had ever known.

DID YOU KNOW?

The sealed envelope

Peking was the creation of Yong Le, the third emperor of the Ming dynasty. When he came to the throne he chose it as the site of his new capital, and in 1404 he set about rebuilding it.

There are many stories about how he came to choose Peking. One is that when he was made emperor he was handed a sealed envelope by a mysterious astrologer.

Emperor Yong Le took a close interest in the planning of the Forbidden City.
He believed that Ming rule would last forever. But by 1644 rivals had taken over, and the
last Ming ruler had killed himself.

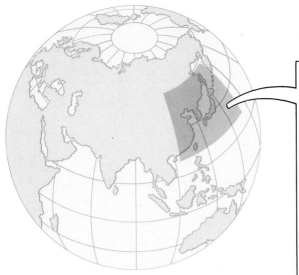
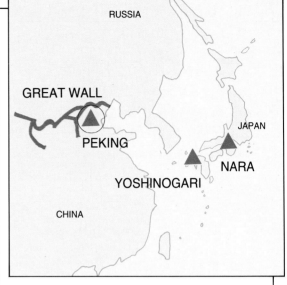

The Forbidden City is in the centre of the modern city of Beijing. It was close to the northern border of the Ming empire. Attacks on China had always come from the north.

When he opened it, he found that it contained detailed plans of the new city. Another story is that the plans were revealed in a dream to the Buddhist monk who had been Yong Le's teacher when he was a boy.

Display of power

The reason for Yong Le's choice was probably more down to earth. Before he became emperor, he had fought many campaigns against rebels and invaders in the north of China, around the Great Wall (see page 21). The Wall is only about 64 kilometres (40 miles) from Peking. It made good sense for the emperor to show his power and authority close to the area where they were most likely to be threatened.

The Forbidden City contained the Imperial Palace, halls where the emperor could receive delegations from within China or from abroad, temples, palaces for each of the emperor's many wives, schoolrooms for his children, and the offices from which China's huge territory was governed. These buildings – mostly of only one or two storeys – were set in elegant squares and courtyards among gardens and ornamental lakes and streams.

Three marble halls

In the largest of the Forbidden City's courtyards are the three great halls of the palace. They stand on terraces of gleaming white marble. Each terrace has a balustrade carved with dragons and other mythical beasts.

The first hall, the Tai He Dian or Hall of Supreme Harmony, was used for the grandest state occasions, such as celebrations of New Year and the emperor's birthday. Three stairways, one of which has a ramp up which the emperor could be carried in his sedan chair, led to the hall. At its entrance the roof was supported by columns, the central six of which were gilded and carved with dragons.

Behind the Tai He Dian was a smaller hall, the Zhong He Dian or Hall of Perfect Harmony. Here, the emperor prepared himself before entering the Tai He Dian.

Finally, there was the Bao He Dian or Hall of the Preservation of Harmony. This was where the emperor received visitors from other countries, scholars and other distinguished Chinese.

The teeming city

The quiet of the Forbidden City, with the emperor's staff and servants quietly going about their business, must have been in sharp contrast to the hubbub of the city outside. Peking was by far the largest and most heavily populated city in China and, at that time, on earth.

From early morning, wagons would arrive from the countryside bringing food and other supplies. There would also be herds of pigs and flocks of sheep, traders bringing goods to market, and people arriving for work in the kitchens, storehouses and offices. They would mingle with elegant nobles arriving for an audience, imperial guards exercising their horses and perhaps some of the emperor's forty-eight elephants being given their morning walk.

Behind the Meridian Gate, the entrance to the Forbidden City, the emperor would hear nothing of this. He lived, with his immediate family, in his own world, far from the everyday lives and concerns of his people.

The Chinese dragon

Images of the dragon, the symbol of the emperor, are to be seen over and over again in the Forbidden City. Marble dragons look out from the terraces of the great halls. Through the centre of the city runs a pathway which has dragons carved into its marble surface. This pathway was regarded as so sacred that only the spirits could use it. The emperor was carried over it in a sedan chair by servants who walked on either side of the sacred stones.

In other cultures the dragon often represents evil. Chinese dragons are different; they breathe fire, and so stand for imperial power. But they are also in charge of bringing the rain, and so they are protective, defending China and its people from starvation.

An imperial dragon.

The Meridian Gate

The Wu Men, as the Chinese called the Meridian Gate, guarded the entrance to the Forbidden City and shut the emperor and his family off from the clamour of the rest of Peking. Only people with permission were allowed to pass through it. Apart from those who worked inside, they would be foreign visitors or Chinese nobles or scholars who had asked for an audience with the emperor. The three great halls where these audiences were held can be seen beyond the gate.

The Wu Men was approached by a marble bridge over the River of Golden Water, one of many canals which added to the beauty of the city and at the same time provided a regular water supply.

The central entrance of the Meridian Gate was for the emperor's own use. He was carried through it on a sedan chair borne by 120

servants, preceded and followed by a vast
procession of attendants and officials.

When visitors from the Western world brought
back descriptions of the Forbidden City, from
about 1600 onwards, they were not believed at
first. The imperial palace and halls were far
more magnificent than the buildings of any
capital city in the West, and no Western ruler
maintained such a huge court.

Much of the splendour of the old city is due to
the fact that it was built in one style so that each
building blends with the next to make a pleasing
whole. Chinese builders used timber frames, with
elaborate frameworks of beams to support the
roofs. They achieved many of their finest effects
by the addition of decorations such as carved
brackets, balustrades and arches, and by
carefully chosen colours.

The imperial home

The emperor and his family lived in three palaces at the heart of the Forbidden City, arranged around an inner courtyard. They had their own temples and bath-houses for ritual cleansing ceremonies, and places for rituals of ancestor worship.

The emperor's own palace was called the Qian Qing Gong, the Palace of Heavenly Purity. It was lavishly decorated with carvings and inlaid images of dragons and other mythical beasts. The centre-piece was a large throne.

After about 1500 the Ming emperors chose to live in smaller palaces in the park, and the Palace of Heavenly Purity became another audience hall.

Marriage rooms

The empress had her own palace, the Kun Ning Gong or Palace of Earthly Tranquillity. This included a smaller area which was used for imperial weddings, with a bedroom where the couple spent the first night of their marriage.

The empress also had a second palace, the Jiao Tai Dian or Hall of Union, which she used as a throne room. Later, this was used as a hall to exhibit relics of past emperors. The theme of the carvings and other decorations in the Empress's palaces was the phoenix, her personal symbol.

Imperial gardens

Beyond the palaces lay the imperial park. This was designed for enjoyment, not for ceremony. There was a collection of exotic trees and other plants, set in a network of patterned paths with fountains, pavilions and pedestals. In winter, when there was no blossom on the trees, a team of women would decorate them with artificial flowers.

No effort was spared to make a walk in the park a constant delight for the imperial family. Bronze incense burners were placed at intervals along the paths to waft sweet scent about the gardens. There were also wind bells to add a gentle, soothing tinkle.

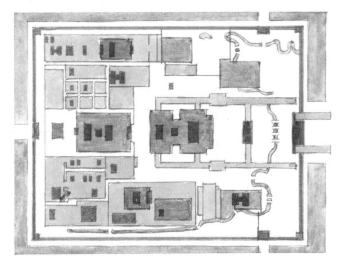

Above: Ground plan of the Forbidden City.
Right: A woman servant spinning silk for robes.

Feng shui

Chinese architects had to worry about more than how a building would look and what materials would be used. They had to design buildings which were in harmony with nature and which would not offend the spirits of earth, water and air. In order to do this, they followed a set of rules called feng shui.

There were strict rules about the way buildings should be positioned, on lines running north to south or east to west. Airy courtyards and gardens, and stretches of water were also part of the scheme.

The rules of feng shui were followed in Yong Le's rebuilding of Peking. Most of the streets run north to south or east to west, and all the major buildings in the Forbidden City are built along a north to south line. Following the rules of feng shui, the Chinese believed, would ensure health and good fortune for the buildings' occupants.

Preparing for a feng shui reading.

Travellers' tales

Chinese civilisation was completely unknown to the Western world until, in 1295, a Venetian merchant returned home after a journey of exploration in Asia. His name was Marco Polo.

People could not believe the stories he told them. He spoke of a great empire ruled by Kublai Khan, who had come from the north to conquer all China, and he described the country's achievements. The people of China used paper and had invented printing. In battle they used rockets filled with an explosive mixture of chemicals called gunpowder. Their knowledge of medicine, science and technology was far ahead of that in Europe.

What Marco Polo had seen was, in fact, the last days of Kublai Khan's rule in China. The great Mongol emperor, who was the grandson of Genghiz Khan, died in 1294, and soon afterwards the Mongol empire in China collapsed.

In 1368 the first of the Ming rulers, Hung Wu, took over. He was a Buddhist monk who had become a soldier and led a campaign to get rid of the Mongols. Yong Le, who rebuilt Peking, was the third Ming emperor. It was not until about 1600, nearly two hundred years later, that Jesuit missionaries of the Roman Catholic Church visited Peking and brought news of its marvels back to the West.

The Taj Mahal

Agra, India, AD 1632–43

*India's most famous building is a jewel-like memorial,
set in a garden of exquisite beauty, built by an emperor of the Mughals
to express his love for his favourite wife.*

Shah Jehan, ruler of the Mughal Empire in India from 1628 to 1658, had many wives, but there was one whom he loved above all others. Her name was Mumtaz Mahal.

She was more than merely his wife and the mother of fourteen of his children. She was also Shah Jehan's closest adviser. Some people said when she married him she became the true ruler of the Mughal Empire. Certainly, she had a great deal of influence on the emperor and played a major part in affairs of state.

She was also known for her kindness to the poor and needy. She had lists made of widows and orphans, and saw that they were well provided for.

Death of an Empress

In 1631, the third year of Shah Jehan's reign, this happy marriage was shattered. The emperor and Mumtaz Mahal had gone together to the Deccan, in the south of their territory, to lead the fight against a rebellion. While there, Mumtaz gave birth to her fourteenth child, a girl.

At first, all was well with both mother and the baby. But then a messenger came to Shah Jehan with the news that Mumtaz was gravely ill. He rushed to her bedside and ordered his team of royal doctors to try to save her life. Sadly, despite all their efforts, nothing could be done and Mumtaz died.

The emperor in mourning

Shah Jehan was almost destroyed with grief. He ordered a two-year period of mourning and, perhaps to keep his mind occupied, began the planning of a mausoleum – a tomb and memorial – for Mumtaz. It was to be called the Taj Mahal, 'the crown of the region', which had been one of Mumtaz's

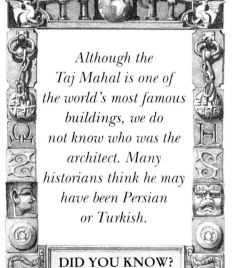

Although the Taj Mahal is one of the world's most famous buildings, we do not know who was the architect. Many historians think he may have been Persian or Turkish.

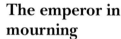

DID YOU KNOW?

The domes and minarets of the Taj Mahal point heavenwards to remind visitors of the woman who inspired its building, Mumtaz Mahal. Her death robbed Shah Jehan of his beloved companion, but gave the world one of its greatest treasures.

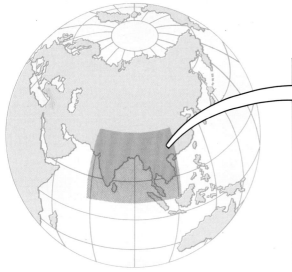

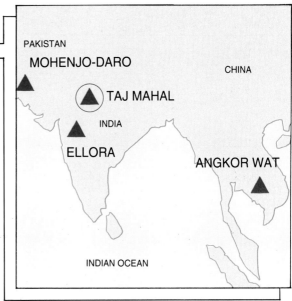

The Taj Mahal is beside the River Jamuna at Agra, about 175 kilometres (115 miles) south of Delhi. Agra was the Mughal capital, founded by Akbar in about 1560.

imperial titles. The Taj Mahal was to be a place of sacred memory – but it was also to be a thing of beauty set in peaceful surroundings.

A 20,000-strong army of workmen was assembled for the project. A special town, Mumtazabad, was built near the site to house them all. A herd of 1000 elephants was used to haul the white marble of which the Taj Mahal was built. Merchants from as far away as Russia, Persia and Tibet arrived bringing precious stones for use in decorating the inside walls. There were craftsmen from Italy, Turkey and France, including a Venetian jeweller called Veroneo and a French goldsmith, Austin of Bordeaux.

Although it was built on the orders of one Mughal emperor, the Taj Mahal was truly an international achievement – a display of the world's skills.

Dome among the trees

The first part of the Taj Mahal the visitor sees is its great white dome, which seems to float above the trees. The Mughals were followers of Islam, and in Islamic art the dome points the way to heaven.

Inside the main gate, the Taj Mahal, on its vast marble terrace, stands out against the sky and is reflected in the simple rectangular pool in front of it. It is a perfectly symmetrical eight-sided building, 57 metres (186 ft) across, crowned by its central dome 24.5 metres (80 ft) high and 15 metres (50 ft) across at its base. There are smaller domes at each corner, and minarets stand at the four corners of the terrace.

Each of these features seems to lead the visitor's eye towards the central dome and so to thoughts of the empress whose memorial this is.

Dazzling details

The beauty of the Taj Mahal is not only in its lines and proportions. The white marble is inlaid with semi-precious stones such as agates, bloodstones and jaspers. There are floral designs, intertwined leaves, wreaths and other patterns.

There is a door on each side of the central mausoleum, with texts from the Koran, the holy book of Islam, over each doorway. They lead to the tomb chamber beneath the great dome.

Mumtaz Mahal's body was buried below the floor of the tomb chamber, and an empty stone coffin, covered with more texts from the Koran in elegant script, marks the spot above where she lies. The tombs were originally surrounded by a screen of solid silver inlaid with precious stones.

Paradise garden

In Islamic tradition gardens represent paradise, and a formal garden, walled with red sandstone, provides the setting for the Taj Mahal.

In Shah Jehan's day the ponds were stocked with ornamental fish, and peacocks and other exotic birds strutted on the paths. Birds of prey were kept away by white-robed guards armed with pea-shooters. The gardens were the place for noble families to gather and relax after they had paid their respects to the memory of Mumtaz.

Companions in death

If Shah Jehan had had his way, the Taj Mahal would have stood beside a second, black mausoleum which he planned to build for his own body. But this was not to be.

In 1658 he fell ill, and his son Aurangzeb forcibly took control of the Mughal Empire. For the last eight years of his life Shah Jehan was virtually his son's prisoner. When he died, he was buried in the Taj Mahal alongside Mumtaz. Perhaps it was right that they should be companions in death as they had been in life.

Four for perfection

In Islamic tradition the number four has a special meaning. It stands for completeness and perfection. This explains the repetition of the number four in the building and surroundings of the Taj Mahal. In turn, this leads to the satisfying balance which makes the mausoleum, even to non-Islamic eyes, look so perfect in its design.

The four domes of the main building and the four minarets at the corners of the terrace

Detail of the Taj's mosaics.

make invisible diagonals that concentrate the visitor's attention on the central dome. There are four doors to the main building, one on each of its four longest sides.

The theme of four is repeated in the layout of the garden. There are four square lawns, each of which is equally divided into sixteen to make a total of sixty-four flower-beds. Each bed contains 400 flowering plants and this design is still followed today.

Shah Jehan

Shah Jehan was the fifth ruler of the Mughal Empire founded by Babur in 1526. He became emperor in 1627 on the death of his father. The Mughals were hungry for more territory, and ruthless in their determination to fight for it. Under Shah Jehan the Mughals pushed their frontiers steadily outwards, particularly in the south.

But Shah Jehan's thirty-year reign was not only one of war. Under his rule, Mughal architecture reached its peak. The Taj Mahal was only one of the buildings he created. He masterminded the Pearl Mosque at Agra, a completely white mosque except for some yellow stone used in the floor and a black inscription. Also at Agra, he rebuilt the Red Fort, replacing much of its red sandstone with white marble. He founded the city of Delhi as well and built a fort and a mosque there.

Preserving Islam

Shah Jehan, a devout Muslim, was determined to impose Islam on the people of his empire. He brutally murdered a group of Portuguese Roman Catholics who had settled in Bengal, for fear they would spread Christianity among his people. In 1632, the year work began on the Taj Mahal, he ordered that no more Hindu temples should be built.

In the end he was overthrown by his son, just as he had, as a young man, led a rebellion against his own father.

Shah Jehan was both a lover and a ruthless warrior.

The Mughal Empire

The Mughal Empire had its beginnings in the high, flat land of Mongolia to the north of China. Around 1200 a strong leader, Genghis Khan, defeated the rulers of various rival tribes and brought Mongolia together as one nation. He then set out on a campaign of conquest.

Within fifty years, the Mongol Empire stretched from the Adriatic Sea in Europe to China in the east, and it included Persia. The Persians called the Mongols 'Mughals' and converted them to Islam. Now, the Mughals themselves began to build an Islamic empire. Between 1526 and 1530 when he died, Babur carved out the Mughal Empire in India.

The Mongols had a reputation as fierce and ruthless people who did not spare their enemies. This tradition carried on with the Mughals. They ruled by terror. There was furious rivalry for the throne, between the generations of Mughal princes, and the history of the empire is one of massacre and torture. Shah Jehan's reign was no less bloodthirsty than any other emperor.

Alongside the Mughal habit of violence went a love of art, music, gardens and architecture. It is odd that the people who brought such pain and destruction to the world should also have left behind some of the finest buildings. The Taj Mahal is just one example.

By 1700 the Mughal Empire stretched almost to the southern tip of India. But one by one its states rebelled against high taxes and the ban on Hinduism. Soon, the empire began to fall apart, and the British arrived to take over India.

Building the Taj

Bringing together the work-force and materials for the Taj Mahal must have been a mammoth operation, comparable with mounting a large military campaign. The Mughals were used to warfare, and no doubt applied the same skills of organisation to building.

Work began in 1632 and continued for the next eighteen years. First, the site had to be cleared. Then the structure of white marble was erected. Finally, teams of craftsmen added the mosaic decorations which give the Taj Mahal its special sparkle.

The finest materials and the most expert craftsmen were brought from all over the Mughal Empire and beyond, including craftsmen from Europe. Nothing but the best, Shah Jehan had decreed, was good enough for his memorial to his beloved wife.

A diagram showing how the Taj was constructed.

Where to go

Although pictures will tell you a lot, it's much better to go to a museum and look at all the things that archaeologists have found from a vanished civilisation. You will get an even better idea of how a people lived and worked and what they thought was important by looking at the statues, jewellery, pottery and other remains.

Some museums have special visiting days when they let you actually touch these ancient things and examine them properly. Often school visits are allowed special access to items which are not usually on display if they are studying a particular period or culture. But **always** check the opening days and times before you try to visit a museum to avoid disappointment.

British museums

The following museums have good general collections on display from some of the civilisations featured in this book:

British Museum, Great Russell St, London WC2 (071–636 1555)

Museum of Mankind, 6 Burlington Gardens, London W1 (071–437 2224)

Victoria & Albert Museum, Cromwell Rd, London SW7 (071–938 8441)

Birmingham Museum & Art Gallery, Chamberlaine Sq, Birmingham (021–253 2834)

Fitzwilliam Museum, Trumpington St, Cambridge (0223–332900)

University Museum of Archaeology and Anthropology, Downing St, Cambridge (0223–337733)

Ashmolean Museum, Beaumont St, Oxford (0865–278000)

Pitt-Rivers Museum, South Parks Rd, Oxford (0865–270927)

Royal Museum of Scotland, Queen St, Edinburgh (031–255 7534)

Glasgow Museum & Art Gallery, Kelvingrove, Glasgow (041–357 3929)

The Burrell Collection, Pollok Country Park, Glasgow G43 (041–649 7151)

Specific sites

Mohenjo-Daro – much of what Sir Mortimer Wheeler found is displayed in a museum at Mohenjo-Daro. There is more to be seen in the Lahore Museum in Lahore, the National Museum of Pakistan in Karachi, Pakistan and the National Museum in Delhi, India.

The Great Wall – there is little excavated material from the Great Wall. You can visit the tomb of Shih-huang-ti at Mount Lishan and see his pottery army.

Yoshinogari – there is a free exhibition at Yoshinogara and the whole site is open to visitors. The best collections of Yayoi material are in the Tokyo National Museum and the Archaeological Museum of Kokugakuin University in Tokyo, Japan.

Ellora – there is little excavated material from Ellora. The National Museum in Delhi has a large collection of material from this period of Indian history.

Nara – the Nara National Museum displays most of the material from this period that is not still in the temples. There is more to be seen in the Tokyo and Kyoto National Museums, Japan.

Angkor – any material remaining in Khampuchea is inaccessible. There is a small collection of material from the Khmer civilisation in the Victoria & Albert Museum (see above) and also in the Louvre Museum in Paris.

Easter Island – there is a museum on Easter Island that contains the best material. There is a statue from Easter Island in the Museum of Mankind (see above).

Great Zimbabwe – most of the finds are in the museum at Great Zimbabwe, Zimbabwe.

The Forbidden City – the whole of this complex is now a museum. Many Chinese art treasures are on display in its various halls, as well as relics of the last emperors of China.

The Taj Mahal – there is no excavated material from the Taj Mahal. The National Museum in Delhi and the museum in Agra display treasures of the Mughal Emperors.

Find out some more:

Civilisations of Asia – Williams, Brian (ed) (Cherrytree Press, 1990)

Everyday Life in Early Imperial China during the Han Period 202 BC–AD 220 – Loewe, Michael (Batsford, 1968)

Indian Folk Tales & Legends – Gray, J.E.B. (Oxford University Press, 1989)

Japan, 5000 BC to Today – Pilbeam, Mavis (Franklin Watts, 1988)

Japanese Folk Tales & Legends – McAlpine, Helen & William (Oxford University Press, 1989)

Let's Go to Zimbabwe – Lye, Keith (Franklin Watts, 1987)

Mahabharata for Children – Nayak, R.S. (ed.) (Ananda Books, 1987)

Rama and Sita – Govinder, Ram (Blackie, 1987)

Ramayana for Children – Nayak, R.S. (ed.) (Ananda Books, 1987)

Adult books you might enjoy:

Aku-Aku – the secret of Easter Island – Heyerdahl, Thor (Unwin Books, 1982)

Angkhor & the Khmers – Macdonald, Malcolm (Oxford University Press, 1987)

Cultural Atlas of China – Blunden & Elvin (Phaidon, 1983)

Easter Island: the mystery solved – Heyerdahl, Thor (Souvenir, 1989)

The Great Wall of China – Schwartz, Daniel (Thames & Hudson, 1991)

The Kon-Tiki Expedition – Heyerdahl, Thor (Unwin Books, 1982)

Zimbabwe Culture: ruins & reaction – Caton-Thompson, Gertrude (Frank Cass, 1971)

Index